What People Are Saying About Anne Prinz and

LIVING YOUR EXCLAMATION POINT LIFE!

"In these challenging times, Anne takes a refreshing look at how you can transform circumstances so you can live a life you would absolutely love living. *Living Your Exclamation Point Life!* is a must read!"

— Mary Morrissey, Founder of the Life Mastery Institute, Best-Selling Author of *No Less Than Greatness* and *Building Your Field of Dreams*

"This book is a gem—a huge contribution and advancement in the art and science of manifestation and transformation. It's right up there with Mary Morrissey and Jack Canfield's writings. Anne Prinz enjoins us to live our precious lives from a place of true power and purpose. Make this book a trusted companion on your own journey to greatness!"

— Beth Beurkens, M.A., Award-Winning Author of *Shaman's Mirror* and *Shaman's Eye*

"*Living Your Exclamation Point Life!* is a fantastic instrument for transforming your circumstances into living a life you love! Anne beautifully teaches you proven principles that will help you achieve the results you've been dreaming of. Two thumbs way up!"

— Mathew Boggs, Director of the Life Mastery Institute and Best-Selling Co-Author of *Project Everlasting*

"This practical, no-nonsense book offers self-help techniques through concise, well-worded advice. It pushes the reader toward taking action, rather than merely toying with intellectual ideas. It's a great teacher for anyone on an inner quest journey."

— Susan Friedmann, CSP, International Bestselling Author of *Riches in Niches: How to Make it BIG in a small Market*

"Wow! Anne Prinz knows how to create her own destiny! When her doctors told her she would never recover from chronic fatigue syndrome, she chose a different destiny and conquered every obstacle in her path. Now she shares all her secrets for how you can also live your exclamation point life!"

— Patrick Snow, Publishing Coach and International Best-Selling Author of *Creating Your Own Destiny* and *Boy Entrepreneur*

"In *Living Your Exclamation Point Life!*, Anne Prinz uses her extensive holistic healthcare background and deep study of universal life principles to provide the reader with clear steps to transcend circumstances and create his or her vision of an abundant life of purpose and happiness. As a Certified Life Mastery Consultant, Anne understands and explains the immense value of mentorship. With her own passion and humor, Anne propels her readers to their success."

— Joan McManus, MA, CCC, CFP, and Author of *Becoming Your Dream: Conceive It, Believe It, Achieve It, Receive It*

"Anne has a keen understanding of the human condition and is an expert at pinpointing the causes behind a person's challenges. I know firsthand how accurate and in-depth her coaching work is. This book will help you significantly improve your results. Run, don't walk to buy it!"

— Tara Brown, Author of *Unleashing Your Inner Beauty*

"*Living Your Exclamation Point Life* is a phenomenal idea. I love the title because it reminds me to live large and embrace everything that life has to offer. Anne Prinz encourages us to find the obstacles stopping us from living large, and she teaches us how to overcome them so we can, like Thoreau, live deliberately and not at the end say that we hadn't lived."

— Tyler R. Tichelaar, PhD and Award-Winning Author of *Narrow Lives* and *The Best Place*

"In *Living Your Exclamation Point Life!*, Anne Prinz reveals that the Universe is waiting to deliver what we want for our lives if we're just open to receiving it. In fact, the truth is that the Universe wants you to succeed, so take Anne's advice. Ask for what you want and add 'This or something better' and then get ready for your life to change."

— Nicole Gabriel, Author of *Finding Your Inner Truth* and *Stepping Into Your Becoming*

"Anne Prinz captures the essence of leading our lives with clarity of purpose to create a life we love. Through stories, she inspires the reader to see how shifting perspective influences and improves lives."

— Diane Albano, EdD, Author of *Nice Has No Voice: Self-Leadership Strategies for Work and Personal Relationships*

"Reading your book gave me great pleasure as it validated so many of my life experiences and opened me to the vulnerability and innocence necessary to continue to pursue life as a man listening to the ever present inner guidance that has been directing me all of my life. Only in my later years has the awareness of this inner guidance become apparent, and your book is a reminder of my experiences, both those pleasant and unpleasant. Thank you for your candor and willingness to expose your life as a way of manifesting grace, dignity, and integrity. You have become the exclamation point you advocate.

My best to you as you continue to manifest your brilliance and humility with light-hearted reverence for your life and as a contribution to others."

— Dr. Robert Brooks, Doctor of Chiropractic

"This book will help you create your best life, regardless of outside circumstances, by awakening your imaginative faculties and strengthening your connection to Source. A summation is beautifully and accurately conveyed by Anne's father: "We are very much like the butterflies…. If we listen, we will know the direction of the path, but then it is up to us to follow." May this book inspire you to create successes in every area of your life."

— Laura Cole, Owner of Inspirational Outcomes

"Having developed wisdom from her connection to Spirit and life experiences, Anne relays how to create a life worth living. Great read!"

— Donna Broadwell, Empowerment Specialist,
Owner of Meta Healing Connections

"Anne Prinz is a gem! She shines light on the path of direction and is always insightful and uplifting in a gentle yet firm manner. I highly recommend Anne to anyone who is seeking a more meaningful and productive life."

— Dr. Jenna Hobbins, Doctor of Chiropractic

"I am truly inspired and motivated by the coaching I am doing with Anne. Her programs have transformed my life. Thank you, Anne, for sharing this work with the world. It is terrific!"

— Julie Macken, Artist and Yoga Instructor

"I highly recommend Anne Prinz as a Life Mastery Consultant. This has been the best move I have made! I am so thankful and grateful for this work. I am dreaming big thanks to Anne and her coaching programs. Anne is loving, patient, and full of insight. She is a person who connects people. Study with Anne and start building your dreams!"

— Darlene Neff, LMT, Myofascial Release Specialist

"Happily, God has blessed this world with some old souls—those who can combine the knowledge gained from experience with the truth of the spirit and share that wisdom to help us on our journey. Anne is one such soul. With grace and humility, she has the ability to dissect a situation to its fundamental elements and offer suggestions that can make profound changes in one's life. She has offered tremendous support and help to me over the years. I know she will do the same for you."

— Connie Lannan, Marketing Manager for a Trade Association

"Anne is a wonderful and deeply supportive lady. When my life was at its worst, she was there with her infectious smile and personal encouragement. Anne sees the more important things in life to focus on. Anyone would be blessed to study with her. Thank you, Anne, for you gave me many moments of light during a confusing and dark time in my life."

— Cynthia Craig, Student in Biblical Counseling

A Success Blueprint for Harnessing Your Full Potential

LIVING YOUR EXCLAMATION POINT LIFE!

How to Transform Your Circumstances and Lead with Vision, Purpose, and Passion

ANNE L. PRINZ

AVIVA PUBLISHING
New York

Living Your Exclamation Point Life!:
How to Transform Your Circumstances and Lead with Vision, Purpose, and Passion

Copyright © 2018 by Anne L. Prinz. All rights reserved.
Published by:

Aviva Publishing
Lake Placid, NY
(518) 523-1320
www.AvivaPubs.com

All Rights Reserved. No part of this book may be used or reproduced in any manner whatsoever without the expressed written permission of the author. Address all inquiries to:

Anne L. Prinz
Telephone: 309-797-4779
Email: Anne@AnneLPrinz.com
www.AnneLPrinz.com
www.LivingYourExclamationPointLife.com
www.ExclamationPointLiving.com

ISBN: 978-1-947937-06-2
Library of Congress Control Number: 2017915741

Editor: Tyler Tichelaar/Superior Book Productions
Cover Designer: Nicole Gabriel/Angel Dog Productions
Interior Book Layout: Nicole Gabriel/Angel Dog Productions
Author Photo: Jaime Hughes

Every attempt has been made to source all quotes properly.
Printed in the United States of America
First Edition
2 4 6 8 10 12

"Follow your bliss, and doors will open for you that you never knew existed.

Follow your bliss and the universe will open doors for you where there were only walls."

— Joseph Campbell

This is to the one…

who is feeling lost and tired,
who is hungry for a life worth living,
who is willing to break free from the past,
who is seeking to discover more meaning in life,
who is being called forth in a new direction,
who is ready to live an ever-abundant life,
who is willing to take the next step,
who is ready to be transformed.

This is for you.

ACKNOWLEDGMENTS

No book is created alone, so I would like to thank the following for their assistance, support, and inspiration in writing *Living Your Exclamation Point Life!*:

Caroline Joy Adams, Diane Albano, Alan Alda, James Allen, Elizabeth Appell, Raymond Charles Barker, Robert Bass, Genevieve Behrend, Roy T. Bennett, Beth Beurkens, Ralph H. Blum, Mathew Boggs, Donna Broadwell, Robert Brooks, DC, Les Brown, Tara Brown, Dan Buettner, Joseph Campbell, Jim Carrey, Alyson Cinquemani, Pema Chödrön, Deepak Chopra, Paulo Coelho, Laura Cole, James C. Collins, Cynthia Craig, Max DePree, Heather Dorniden, Jeffrey Dyer, Dr. Wayne Dyer, Amelia Earhart, Thomas Edison, Ralph Waldo Emerson, Tom Fitzgerald, Foundation for Inner Peace, Emmet Fox, Viktor Frankl, Susan Friedmann, Nicole Gabriel, Johann Wolfgang von Goethe, Valerie J. Guastadisegni, Chris Guillebeau, Mark Victor Hansen, Coleman Harris, Olly Hermon-Taylor, Napoleon Hill, Jenna Hobbins, DC, David Icke, Gerald Jampolsky, MD, Katrina Kenison, Elisabeth Kübler-Ross, George Land, Connie Lannan, Susan Lighter, Craig Lounsbrough, Julie Macken, Maxwell Maltz, Chuck Mangione, Jenny Marchal, Greg McKeown, Cheryl McMahill, Joan McManus, Stavros Mento, DC, Victoria Meyn, Dan Millman, Julie Morgenstern, Mary Morrissey, M. Ted Morter, Jr., DC, Oriah Mountain Dreamer, Craig Murray, Ed Mutum, Darlene Neff, Isaac Newton, Anaïs Nin, Harvey Prinz, Jennifer Prinz, Kathryn Prinz, Ruth Prinz, Nibo Qubein, Rasha, Cheryl Richardson, Eleanor Roosevelt, Theodore Roosevelt, Jim Roan, Susan Schabilion, Lisa Shaffer, Derek Sivers, Janet Stessl, Patrick Snow, Socrates, Roy Sweat, DC, Tomy Temerson, Henry David Thoreau, Tyler Tichelaar, Brian Tracy, Mark Twain, Wallace Wattles, Kirsten Wells, Marianne Williamson, Oprah Winfrey, and all the others who have blessed me with their presence on my journey.

CONTENTS

Introduction:	Opening the Door to Your Exclamation Point Life	15
Chapter 1:	Shifting Your Perspective on Circumstances	19
Chapter 2:	Transforming Circumstances into Your Opportunities	33
Chapter 3:	Setting Yourself Free	49
Chapter 4:	Discovering What Is Emerging in You	65
Chapter 5:	Daring to Dream by Defining What You Want	77
Chapter 6:	Trying Your Dream on for Size	91
Chapter 7:	Embracing What's Emerging in You	103
Chapter 8:	Taking a Leadership Role in Systematically Advancing Your Dream	119
Chapter 9:	Creating Your Dream Team	137
Chapter 10:	Empowering Yourself Through Mentorship	145
Chapter 11:	Stepping Forward with Confidence	157
Chapter 12:	Looking to the Past with a Kind Glance	169
Chapter 13:	Letting Go of What No Longer Supports You	187
Chapter 14:	Trusting Your Intuition and Imagining Your Way to Success	201
Chapter 15:	Seizing Your Opportunities	213

A Final Note: Continuing Forward Momentum and Succeeding in Your Vision	225
About the Author	229
About Coaching with Anne L. Prinz	231
Book Anne L. Prinz to Speak at Your Next Event	233

INTRODUCTION

OPENING THE DOOR TO YOUR EXCLAMATION POINT LIFE

"Give time, give space to sprout your potential. Awaken the beauty of your heart—the beauty of your spirit. There are infinite possibilities."

— Amit Ray

Are you overwhelmed and feeling stuck? Are you exhausted from working long hours and not feeling fulfilled by what you do? Does your relationship always seem to be on the back burner, or has it lost its sparkle? Are you struggling to make ends meet and can't figure out how to change your circumstances? Are you concerned about your health but don't feel you have the time or money to get help? Are you about ready to give up on ever living the life of your dreams—your exciting, exclamation point life?

I understand what you are going through. At one time, I feared if something didn't change, I would not live to see another year.

My life was enveloped with circumstances. I felt like the proverbial hamster on a hamster wheel—running all the time but not getting anywhere. I was stuck in the well-worn ruts of my life. It was at this crossroads moment that I took a stand and said, "This year, I am creating a better life for myself." I knew that meant I needed to start looking at my life in a way I had never done before. That choice began turning the tide in my life as I began changing my old patterns, embracing new beliefs, and surrounding myself with people who were already successful in ways I wanted to be.

So, what does it mean to live your exclamation point life? It means creating and living the best life you can dream of; it is about reaching for the stars and attaining them; it is about playing full out; it is about showing up and giving it your best even when things try to hold you back; it is about living a life without the boundaries of conformity, but mostly, it is about living the life you were truly born to live, by awakening to your potential and ultimately sharing the gifts you came to give the world in the way only you can.

In this book, you will learn to shift your perspective so you can change the outcome of circumstances and transform them into opportunities. You will also begin to recognize what is holding you back, what you can do to repattern your old beliefs, and how you can set yourself free from the hold they have on you. You will learn how to look to your past experiences with a kind glance and learn what true forgiveness is all about. By letting go of what you have outgrown, you will learn how to say yes to what you truly would love in your life, discover what is worth transforming, and determine what is worth letting go of.

Something greater is within you, calling you forth to live your greater potential and purpose. In this book, you will learn how to take a deep dive and dare to dream the life you would passionately love to live. You will learn the steps to advance your vision with confidence, even in the midst of circumstances. You will learn how to use your imaginative process along with your intuition to help you create your success. Plus, you will learn the importance of empowering yourself through mentorship and what a mentor means in the success of creating your dream. If you apply the wisdom, experience, skills, and tools offered in this book to your life, you will have learned how to transform your circumstances and lead a life filled with vision, purpose, and passion.

I am the owner of Exclamation Point Living, LLC and a certified Life Mastery Consultant/Life Coach through the Life Mastery Institute. I have been coaching people in health and lifestyles since 1996. I specialize in helping my clients create their exclamation point lives by harnessing their potential and transforming their circumstances.

I enjoy learning and love sharing what I learn with others. Life is a journey, and like you, I continue to evolve, grow, and learn new things. Here I am sharing with you what I have learned in my journey. Each client, organization, and business I work with helps broaden and deepen my understanding. No matter who you are, there is always more to learn, and I look forward to learning with you.

I understand why you have not pursued all your dreams and are not living the life you thought you would be living by now. You may already have a good life, but you are longing for something more. Or perhaps circumstances have gotten in your way and you are experiencing longing and discontent. You may be a single parent, working several jobs to make ends meet, or you may have too many demands on your time. I want you to know that is okay. No matter what you are going through, I believe in you and your ability to transform the circumstances in your current life so you, too, can live your exclamation point life.

This book includes exercises to help you create a life you will love living with space provided to write your thoughts. I recommend you also get a notebook for extra space to write in. This is your time to transform your life so you want to have the best experience this book can offer you.

I want to be your mentor, your accountability partner—the person who stands by your side and helps you navigate the gap from where you are to the dream life you want to live. The one you can count on to help you move past circumstantial living to creating a life by design. I want to be the resource you look toward to help you overcome anything that stands between you and your exclamation point life.

Are you ready to begin stepping into the life that has been waiting for you? Are you ready to expand your comfort zone and step into the new person you are becoming? Are you ready to draw the line in the sand and say, "This is my time. This is my life. I am ready"? If so, I congratulate you for taking this first step forward. I am here to walk with you. Let's start this journey together! You are entering the beginning of the best part of your life! Let's jump in!

Anne A. Pring

CHAPTER 1

SHIFTING YOUR PERSPECTIVE ON CIRCUMSTANCES

"Your present circumstances don't determine where you can go; they merely determine where you start."

— Nibo Qubein

In this chapter, we will cover how shifting your perspective can alter the outcome of circumstances. You do not have to be a victim of circumstance. Instead, you have the choice not to let circumstances get the better of you.

RISING ABOVE YOUR CIRCUMSTANCES

Do you find that circumstances seem to be dictating your life and holding you back? What if you knew you had a choice to change the outcome of circumstances? Do you think that would be beneficial to you?

In my experience, you can rise above any circumstance, but most people do not realize they have a choice. By shifting your perspective, you open the door to changing the outcome of circumstances. In fact, Holocaust survivor and author Viktor E. Frankl, in his book *Man's Search for Meaning*, writes: "The last of human freedoms—the ability to choose one's attitude in a given set of circumstances, to choose one's own way."

I would like to share a story with you of how I rose above a circumstance in my life. It was a warm and sunny, summer afternoon. I had decided it was a good time to go for a walk. Dressed in my shorts and a short-sleeve shirt, I grabbed my cell phone and earbuds so I could listen to an online class. As I headed out on my walk, I was grateful for the perfect afternoon and the opportunity to listen to my class.

About two minutes into my walk, something to my left caught my attention. It was a pit bull terrier, baring his teeth and running straight at me to attack. Immediately, fear penetrated my entire being, and many things went through my head all at the same time. How was I going to defend myself from attack?

In that moment, I made a choice. I chose love over fear, and I chose to fill myself with as much love as possible. I continued to walk confidently forward while at the same time choosing to use techniques I have used for years to help relieve stress and fill my heart with love.

I had learned a stress technique years ago, called loving symbol work, and by keeping my thumb and index finger together while thinking of the most beautiful place in nature, I instantly began to feel calm.

Simultaneously, I started singing the word HU (pronounced hue). A friend of mine taught me to sing this years ago as a love song to God. As I sang loudly, I could feel a wave of peace come over me as I put as much love into it as I could.

A very interesting thing occurred as the dog ran up to me; he began to slow down. He ran in front of me, and as he turned toward me, he had a look of confusion on his face. I continued to walk confidently, holding my loving symbol and singing HU. What I didn't know until that moment was that a second pit bull terrier was planning to attack me—the other dog came from behind me and around my other side. As fear tried to well up in me again, I became more convicted than ever to keep putting as much love into the situation as I could. As the second dog came in front of me, he too looked very confused.

The two dogs then looked at each other as if they thought they were going to do something to me, but they just couldn't remember what that was. They decided to turn in the direction of the path I was walking, and both happily trotted down the path. Once they had turned around the bend in the road and were out of sight, I stopped, bent to my knees, took a great big breath, and stood there for a moment in deep awe and gratitude for what had just transpired.

So what had just happened? Or should I say, what had not happened?

In the middle of a circumstance, I had chosen to rise above it and not accept impending doom as my answer. I chose to create an outcome by design instead of by default. Although many things had been going through my head when I saw the first dog, I never allowed myself to accept a negative outcome. In that moment, I used the tools that came to my mind first. The tools I used had been in my toolbox for many years. So, in that moment of extreme fear, I made a conscious choice to shift my perspective and rely on tools I had often used before to help me reduce stress and fill my heart with love. As the Bible states, "There is no fear in love, but perfect love casts out fear. For fear has to do with punishment, and whoever fears has not been perfected in love" (1 John 4:18).

Every one of us has the possibility to create a life and outcome by design rather than by default; the choice is ours. We also have the choice to develop tools to help us rise above the circumstances in our lives. This book's purpose is to help you recognize and develop skills to create your exclamation point life.

EXERCISE

What circumstance do you currently have in your life where changing your perspective could change your outcome?

_____

_____

_____

_____

If you could change the outcome of those circumstances, what would that look like and what would you choose to do?

_____

_____

_____

_____

What step can you take today to change the outcome of your circumstances so they are determined by design instead of default?

_____

_____

_____

NOTICE WHAT YOU'RE NOTICING

One of my favorite mentors, founder of Life Mastery Institute, Mary Morrissey, taught me the importance of "Notice what you're noticing." To begin understanding this advice, notice the tip of your nose, notice your chin, notice your right knee, notice your left knee, and notice how the air in the room feels on your exposed skin.

Notice that you have an observer self that can focus your attention wherever you place it. This is called mindfulness—being aware and being present in the moment.

In one of my favorite blogs by Morrissey, she writes:

> It's being present enough to notice being *alive*, and to choose the way you experience life…. If I'm walking down the street, feeling crowded by the hustle and bustle and bothered by people bumping into me, I may start to feel irritated. If I notice that irritation and focus on it, that focus will cause the negative feeling to grow. But if I practice mindfulness, I can notice that I'm in a negative, contractive state of mind that's creating a negative experience. I can't control everything around me, but I can control what I'm thinking about everything around me.

In the situation Morrissey describes, you could just as easily choose a more expansive view by noticing the feeling of the warm sunlight on your face and smelling the fragrant flowers in the baskets as you walk by. You can choose to have a different outcome to the same circumstances. The more you choose empowering or expansive thoughts over disempowering, contractive thoughts, the better you are able to rise above circumstances and create the life you desire.

Remember, you always have a choice. By choosing empowering thoughts more often, you are on your way to creating your exclamation point life.

EXERCISE

Are your current thoughts more empowering or disempowering?

_____

What tools can you create to help you "notice what you're noticing" more frequently and choose to create a more empowering view?

_____

_____

_____

SECOND TIME IS A CHARM

Les Brown, one of the greatest motivational speakers of all time, once said, "You cannot expect to achieve new goals or move beyond your present circumstances unless you change."

Every once in a while, life gives us a grand opportunity to learn some big lessons. At a seminar I attended, for our group project we were told to create a tower out of fifty pieces of spaghetti and two rolls of masking tape. The goal was to make it as tall as we could to support an egg for ten seconds. Each team had six members, and we were given fifteen minutes to create our design.

Our team went right to work. Because I have a background in architecture, the group followed my design strategy. We ended up coming in third place with our twenty-nine-inch tower.

When we completed our design and looked up to see what others were doing, it was amazing to see the wide variety of possibilities. Some teams had a scout to see what other teams were doing before their team started to build; another team had only leaders and no one wanted to follow, so their egg never made it off the ground.

And then there was ours. Our tower was so sturdy that the tower would have held the egg for the whole week. But that was not the goal. The goal was to have it as tall as possible to hold the egg for ten seconds.

I realized I led my team with the best idea I could think of in the moment, but my thinking mind alone led my group astray. We could have built the tower higher. The tower only needed to hold the egg for ten seconds, not a whole week.

After reviewing everyone's project and gaining a new perspective on the goal, we were given a second chance.

The team next to us had won the first round, but it had run out of tape to create anything bigger and better. Its members came to my team and said, "Why don't we join forces?" so we did. We combined the two projects. When listening to the instructions the second time, we had a different level of awareness. We were told we could use anything on top of our table, so we used the tablecloth to build our platform one foot taller. Our project ended up being fifty-seven inches tall with tape streamers all around the table to hold up the structure. When testing the egg, the tower lasted about fifteen seconds before collapsing to the ground. The second time was a charm. We succeeded in making the tallest tower in the room.

So what was the difference between the first and second time?

The first time, our thoughts were disempowered, not knowing how strong spaghetti, tape, and an egg could be. Self-importance or lack of it was creating tension in the group. We lacked experience, and we were trying to use our own brain power to make something happen; that something was less than the scope of what was expected in the directions.

The second time, we had more awareness than our previous experience, so we knew more was possible, and we were more confident. In combining our efforts, we all dove in and decided to put our two projects together on a new platform. Everyone was involved and just started taping everything together. Our twelve team members had individual roles, and we all empowered each other. It was exciting to see what we could do once we used our new awareness and allowed the creative spirit of empowerment to enter the equation. As a bonus, it was much more fun than the first time because we fully worked as a team.

EXERCISE

List three events from your life that have seemed disempowering.

_____

_____

_____

What would you do to empower each of those situations if you gave it a second try?

_____

_____

_____

_____

_____

_____

CREATING EMPOWERED MENTAL HABITS

It is so important to protect your mind and what goes into it from negative self-talk and negative energy. In fact, transcendentalist author Ralph Waldo Emerson, warned: "Stand guard at the portal of your mind." Furthermore, in his book *Keys to Success*, Napoleon Hill writes: "Doers take possession of their minds through self-discipline. They make plans, and they carry them out. They direct their minds toward the objects of their desire, and they keep their minds occupied with those things. They don't spend time thinking about what they don't want."

Napoleon is right: We can use our mind to rise above circumstance. By staying focused on the outcome we desire, we can bring it about. We need to start with an idea of what we want, then focus on that desire. We take action while focusing on our desire. We stay mindful that our mind needs to stay positive, and we do not allow it to slip into thinking about what we don't want.

Just imagine what would have happened to me if, when confronted by the two pit bull terriers, I had allowed my mind to slip into thinking about what I didn't want.

EXERCISE

List times when you placed your focus on what you desired and did not let anything stand in your way.

_____

_____

Have there been times when you took your mind off your desire and let it get caught up in the circumstance, thus preventing you from fulfilling your desire? List them.

_____

_____

What action steps can you take to help you make better choices when creating what you desire?

_____

_____

LEARNING THROUGH TURBULENCE

On a flight headed for Dallas, I took the opportunity to rest. Very quickly into the flight, we hit a lot of turbulence. Although I had my seatbelt on, I woke when I was nearly flung from my seat and then yanked right back down by my seatbelt. The woman behind me screamed, and her seat partner calmed her down by reassuring her we were going to be okay.

To get out of the extreme turbulence, the pilot had to change our course a bit. He had to fly above the storm front we were moving through. At one point, the turbulence became so bad again that I had to grab the armrest to remain seated. The pilot again made adjustments to navigate the storm front we were encountering.

When things calmed down, I looked out my window and noticed we were flying on the edge of the storm front. No longer in the turbulence of the unknowing clouds, I now had a clearer view—the storm was in the distance and I was flying in clear skies.

What happens when turbulence comes into our lives? Do we hold the course with what we know and hope the turbulence will just go away? Or, like my pilot, do we adjust our course? Do we make choices to rise above the circumstance of turbulence?

Do circumstances control you, or do you have control over your circumstances? At any given time, circumstances will bring turbulence into your life. To avoid being a victim of circumstance, you must pause, recognize the feelings associated with the turbulence, and then make choices so you can course-correct. You course-correct by becoming present in the moment and going within to listen to your intuition. By doing so, you will be shifting your perception and will become open to fresh ideas, which will help you rise above the circumstances and empower you with new choices.

My pilot saw the turbulence coming and adjusted our course. Even though we could not see through the clouds creating the turbulence, the pilot had tools to help him navigate us out of the storm front. When the pilot's original plan was not enough to get us out of the turbulence, he came up with another plan—a new course of action.

If he had acted as if the turbulence were not there, what do you think would have happened? Might the turbulence have increased with worse effects? The longer we ignore something that is creating turbulence in our life, the more the volume will increase until we pay attention and do something to change our course. Turbulence in our lives can show up as a wake-up call that something is out of balance. It can show up as feelings of longing or discontent. When either of these feelings arise, something inside of you is looking to change. Then it is time to course-correct.

EXERCISE

What turbulence are you experiencing in your life that could be improved with a course correction?

SHIFTING YOUR PERSPECTIVE ON CIRCUMSTANCES

_____

_____

If you could change that circumstance into something you would love, what would it be?

_____

_____

SUMMARY

To shift your perspective when circumstances come into your life, push the pause button and ask yourself, "What is the desired outcome I would like from this circumstance?" In my situation with the pit bull terriers, I knew I wanted to be healthy and whole and continue going on a walk.

Notice what you're noticing—do you always react a certain way when circumstances arise? How could you shift your perception of what you are noticing into a positive outcome?

When you start developing your new tools, you may not have your best results at first, but with awareness, practice, and a willingness to learn, you will develop stronger and more productive tools to assist you.

Learning to self-discipline your mind is important; practice focusing on the thing you want to create and learn ways to stop yourself when you start focusing on what you don't want.

Turbulence is going to show up, and it can create a haze of unknowingness around us. By developing our tools, we can navigate life's storms and get ourselves to the clear skies of our desires; we simply have to be able to course-correct when necessary to get us to our desired destinations.

CHAPTER 2

TRANSFORMING CIRCUMSTANCES INTO YOUR OPPORTUNITIES

"Nothing is predestined. The obstacles of your past can become the gateways that lead to new beginnings."

— Ralph H. Blum

In the last chapter, you learned that you can shift your perspective on circumstances. In this chapter, you will learn how you can transform your circumstances into opportunities. Honor where you are and know you are greater than your circumstances. Let me define "transform" for you. According to Webster's Dictionary, transform means, "to change (something) completely and usually in a good way." What this means is when you take something that once was a circumstance and transform it into an opportunity, you will have "completely" left behind the challenge you have carried with the circumstance, and will be fully able to embrace the opportunity the circumstance has given you. You are then transformed by the process.

LEARNING ABOUT YOUR GENIUS

In 1968, George Land, a general systems scientist, was contacted by NASA to create a study to test creativity. NASA wanted the most creative people to work for it. After creating this test, a thought came to Mr. Land: *What would happen if we tested children to find out about their creativity?* The test followed 1,600 children between the ages of four and five for the next ten years. The results were quite astonishing.

Ninety-eight percent of the children were initially at a genius level. By the time the children turned ten, their genius level had decreased to 32 percent. By the time the children turned fifteen, their genius level had decreased to 10 percent. Adults over the age of twenty only showed a 2 percent genius level with creativity.

So, what happened to us if we were born geniuses?

In a 2010 TEDx speech, Land stated that once we started formal education, we were taught to have convergent and divergent thinking simultaneously. Convergent thinking is the judging, criticizing, censoring part of the mind, and divergent thinking is our imagination, our ability to dream.

Land's study reveals that we are all born geniuses in our ability to dream and create, but once we start listening to those around us, we are taught to judge, criticize, and censor ourselves and others. We become indoctrinated in fear of failure, lack of self-confidence, pressure to conform, dependence on others, etc. We start listening to the voices that would say, "That's a dumb idea!"; "That's not practical!"; "You can't do that!", etc.

According to Land, this condition as an adult is completely reversible, but we must get back to dreaming and not allow the critical voice to determine the outcome of our dreaming.

We have the opportunity to take another look at the circumstances in our lives. How we react to our circumstances comes from years of trained responses. What if, instead, when we are faced by a circumstance, we go into that place of noticing what we are noticing before we respond with the same pattern we have used in the past? What if we take some time to pause? What if we take time to be creative in the moment before we judge the moment? What if we start looking for what is positive in the circumstance? What if we start looking for the opportunities when the circumstances come?

The choice is yours to make. Your dream is waiting for you to discover it once again with childlike wonder.

EXERCISE

What are some circumstances you have judged in the past?

_____

_____

_____

Looking back at those circumstances, what could you have changed by taking time to pause before judging the situation and, instead, choosing to look for the opportunity? What kind of creative solution might you have come up with?

_____

_____

RECOGNIZING THE SELF-CRITICAL MIND

Circumstances can sometimes sneak up on us so quietly that we don't even recognize we have limited the opportunity waiting for us.

I experienced how I can limit my opportunity when I was first introduced to the concert zither, a German folk instrument. My dad had just finished publishing some articles for the newly formed German American Heritage Center in Davenport, Iowa. Someone had donated a picture to the center labeled, "Davenport Zither Club 1885." As editor for the center's newsletter, *Infoblatt*, my dad did research that led him and my mom to Chicago to meet with members of the Chicago Zither Club.

Two players from the Chicago Zither Club came to our new center to play their zithers for a standing-room-only crowd. My mother made sure we got there early so we had front row seats; I was sitting only five feet from the performers.

I was quite mesmerized by the performers as I watched their fingers play the forty-two strings with ease to create such beautiful music.

At the end of the concert, the program director passed around a sign-up paper for anyone interested in learning to play the zither. I passed on signing up by telling myself, "I can't do that; I'm too busy." I did, however, talk to the woman playing the zither. She explained her instrument to me in detail. When I asked her how much a starter zither would cost, she told me, "About $600." I allowed my judgmental voice to stop me when it said, "You can't spend that kind of money on something you may never learn how to play. You already have other hobbies you are no longer doing, so why start something new? You tried playing a stringed instrument in the past and that didn't go very well. Besides, you're a busy person. You just don't have the time." Recognize that kind of self-talk?

TRANSFORMING CIRCUMSTANCES INTO YOUR OPPORTUNITIES

The self-critical part of my mind had just completely rationalized why I should not learn how to play the zither, which I was completely captivated by. At the time, I did not recognize the circumstantial thinking nor how the critical part of my mind was working hard to keep me in a place it considered "safe." In that moment, I let the self-limiting part of my brain win. After all, its message seemed logical based on past and current circumstances. What I completely negated in the moment was my creative side that was totally fascinated by the zither. I shut down the part of me that wanted to get my fingers on the strings and learn how to play the beautiful music I had just heard.

It wasn't until four years later, after attending multiple zither concerts, that one circumstance changed and my longing to play the zither became stronger than the self-critical part of my mind. I will share more on that later in Chapter 7.

The point of this story is how, in all the seemingly quiet circumstances that arise in our lives, the self-critical part of our mind holds us back from doing something we would love. In my case with the zither, I had a second chance, but what about all those times my mind discounted something that could have led to awesome opportunities?

Here is where "notice what you're noticing" becomes so important. Whenever you feel yourself limiting, constricting, or judging a circumstance, if you can catch yourself in the moment, you have the option to push your internal pause button on the self-critical part of your mind. Once paused, you have an incredible opportunity with the choice you make. Ask yourself, "What would be fulfilling and expansive in this moment? What would I love?"

Pausing the self-critical part of your mind is the key to opening the doors of opportunity for you. It will lead you to greater awareness and a much more rewarding life.

EXERCISE

List some circumstances where your self-critical mind has held you back?

_____

_____

What opportunities might have existed in those circumstances if you had hit the pause button on your self-critical mind?

_____

_____

_____

What previous opportunities could still be implemented now?

_____

_____

_____

What are some lessons you can learn from this new understanding that will help you in future circumstances?

_____

_____

_____

CHANGING THE STORIES YOU TELL YOURSELF

In her book *A Return to Love,* Marianne Williamson writes:

> Our deepest fear is not that we are inadequate. Our deepest fear is that we are powerful beyond measure. It is our light, not our darkness that most frightens us. We ask ourselves, "Who am I to be brilliant, gorgeous, talented, and fabulous?" Actually, who are you not to be? You are a child of God. Your playing small does not serve the world.

Williamson is here giving us the opportunity to see who we truly are. We are not the limited people we try to convince ourselves we are. Quite the contrary. We are unlimited in our potential of who we are and what we can create in this life. Your observer self, otherwise known as your higher self or intuitive self, is the part of you that knows we are "powerful beyond measure." This part of us is infinite and contains all possibility. The human side of our nature tries to keep everything inside a set of boundaries. It doesn't want to change, so it will constantly try to stop us from growing. Thus, as we try to grow, the self-critical mind will speak even louder to us to keep us in the old patterns and our comfort zone.

The spiritual, infinite side of our nature is always trying to express more through us. Our life has all the makings of being a magical dance between the infinite and human sides of our nature. When we let go of self-limiting beliefs and allow ourselves to be present in the moment, those two sides of our nature are able to create a life much greater than we may currently imagine.

EXERCISE

What are you noticing about yourself when you set aside the limited views you have in some areas of your life?

_____

_____

_____

Are you finding something of a creative nature wants to be expressed through you? If so, what is it?

_____

_____

_____

FACING BIG CIRCUMSTANCES WITH A FLASHLIGHT OF CURIOSITY

I thought I was on top of the world. Everything was going well. I was a budding young architect, having great success working in New York and Baltimore. The buildings I worked on were receiving awards and being written about in national magazines and a book. My bosses loved my work ethic, and even though I was young, they gave me the responsibility of heading up the Computer Aided Drafting (CAD) for the largest project our office had ever done.

Then on December 9, I came down with what I thought was the flu going around the office. I kept trying to go to work, even though I felt lousy. Fortunately, I had taken some time off work for the holidays, so I tried to recover at my folks' house, but I just couldn't shake it. I tried to return to work after the holidays, but I could only manage working until January 9. That's when the person in our human resources department told me I had used up all my sick leave but I shouldn't come back until I was well. What I didn't know was that would be my last day working in an architectural firm, just four months away from taking my architectural licensing exam.

I went from one infection straight into another. I tried to study for my exams, but I couldn't remember what I was reading. I could only sleep. In February, I went to stay with my parents again. That was when my aunt mentioned she had read an article about chronic fatigue syndrome; its symptoms seemed to describe what I was experiencing. When I returned home, my doctor diagnosed me with chronic fatigue syndrome and tried to help me get better.

Regardless, my health severely deteriorated. At times, it took everything I had to heat up a bowl of Campbell's soup, only to have to lay my head on the table between swallows of soup. I was limited to driving seven miles and I carried a list of friends' phone numbers on the back of my driver's license in case I got lost and could not find my way home. One time at the dentist's office, I was unable to remember how to write my name. It felt like I was living a nightmare, or was I?

Very early in my illness, I knew I was not going to get well until I learned what it was meant to teach me. At first, I fought it by trying to study for my exams and work from home, but that was just not possible. I finally surrendered, not to the illness pattern, but to the way I was facing the circumstance. Deep within me, I knew this illness was providing me with a great gift, so it was up to me to discover it and unfold its mysteries.

Instead, I became curious. I journaled daily to see whether there were patterns I could begin to understand. I had to sleep a tremendous amount and had very little energy, so I became mindful of how I was using the precious energy I had. As a result, I learned how to turn to others for help and how to be a good listener; I developed a depth to my relationships I had not known before. Each day, I learned to be more present in the moment and how to take the step I could with what I had.

During this time, I also learned how to do new things that would allow me to feel I had accomplished something each day. A friend and I learned how to quilt by hand just like our grandmothers had done. I even entered a cross-stitch competition after designing a scissors case for a cross-stitch magazine; ultimately, I had my design published. I also became a contact for the CFIDS (Chronic Fatigue Immune Dysfunction Syndrome) Association and was glad to meet others who were curious like me.

But mostly, people were surprised that I could keep such a positive attitude through everything. I chose not to dwell on what I could not do; instead, I focused on what I could do with what I had so I could make a difference in the world. Although I had to sleep fourteen hours per day, my illness did not own me. It may have greatly affected my physical being, but it could not touch the spiritual side of me that was growing by leaps and bounds by remaining curious.

Four years into being sick, a renowned doctor told me the good news and the bad news. After all his testing, the good news was I didn't have anything worse, and the bad news was because of how long I had been sick, I would never recover or be able to work again. When he told me that, I thought, "Wow, he doesn't know me very well!" This was a decisive moment for me in harnessing my thinking power to create a new result. In that moment, I went from asking myself, "What can I do to manage my illness better?" to asking an empowered question of "What can I do to get well so I can work again?" My internal response to the doctor shifted my thinking from circumstance thinking into empowered thinking—creating a life I would love, simply by changing the daily question I was asking myself. By changing this daily question, things started shifting around me and doors started to open that would lead to my recovery. I knew the circumstance did not have me. I just needed to be open to the answers the gift of illness had come to give me. I had too much life left to live, and a lot of life yet to give.

The biggest door opened for me the day of my older sister's wedding. I was sitting at a table with her chiropractor, and to make small talk, I said, "I have a friend who works for a chiropractor who does the same type of chiropractic you do." When I told her his name, her eyes nearly bulged out of her head; she pointed her finger at me and said, "Don't you think twice about it; you go see him." Her response was so strong that I knew I needed to follow through with what she had said.

I made an appointment the day I got back, and the moment I shook my new chiropractor's hand, I knew my life would be transformed forever.

Remember Webster Dictionary's definition of transform? I was changed completely. I never doubted I would get well. I simply knew that first I needed to learn fully the gift the illness came to teach me. I learned there was another side to me—a side not touched by circumstance. A side that was "powerful beyond measure."

Circumstances do not happen to us. They happen for us so we can gain the gifts they are there to teach. All of life is here to teach us if we are willing to listen and learn. In honoring the gift of circumstance, we evolve beyond our previous limitations into a new and expanded way of living.

EXERCISE

What is a circumstance in your life that feels big?

_____

_____

_____

What would be some possible outcomes if you surrendered your struggle with the circumstance and became curious about new possibilities?

_____

_____

_____

Name some possible gifts the circumstance came to teach you?

_____

_____

_____

What are some possible opportunities of this circumstance, or what are some empowering questions you can ask?

_____

_____

_____

Remember, the quality of your life does not need to be dictated by your circumstances. You can choose whether or not the circumstance will control you or be a teacher so you can move forward.

CHOOSING EMPOWERED THINKING

James Allen was a British philosophical writer and a pioneer of the self-help movement. His best-known work, *As a Man Thinketh,* was published in 1903. Allen writes:

> They themselves are makers of themselves by virtue of the thoughts which they choose and encourage; that mind is the master weaver, both of the inner garment of character and the outer garment of circumstances, and that, as they may have hitherto woven in ignorance and pain they may now weave in enlightenment and happiness.

Allen is teaching that *you* are the one who has power over your own thoughts. You can choose to live in "ignorance and pain," or you can choose to create "enlightenment and happiness." The "inner garment of character" is your intuitive self, the part of you that can "notice what you're noticing" and make a shift in your perception. The "outer garment of circumstances" is what happens outside of you as part of the physical nature you experience. This combination of your intuitive self and your physical nature in the present moment gives you the greatest opportunity for growth. Whereas before you may have created negative situations for yourself due to your own perceptions, now you can create an illuminated way of thinking that brings your life greater joy.

No one can ever choose an illuminated way of thinking for you. It is a choice you work on each day to encourage the collaboration of the intuitive self and your physical nature. By remaining mindful to trust your intuitive side, you will be guided to the best possible outcomes.

EXERCISE

When have you seen your intuitive self bring an awareness that supported your physical nature?

_____

_____

_____

What step can you take that would encourage you to collaborate more between your intuitive self and your physical nature within your current circumstances?

_____

_____

_____

TRANSFORMING CIRCUMSTANCES INTO YOUR OPPORTUNITIES

SUMMARY

From the George Land study, we understand that as children, we began listening to those around us. By the time we were school age, we had learned to judge, criticize, and censor ourselves and others. We developed a fear of failure, lack of self-confidence, pressure to conform, and dependence. With this new input, we began to believe our self-critical nature was true as opposed to us truly being the creative geniuses we were at birth.

It is up to us to start recognizing our self-critical mind. We can do so by using our noticing skills to shed light on the blind spots we created when we developed our self-critical mind. By turning on the light of awareness, we can start transforming our old patterns to move beyond the limitation of circumstances and free ourselves to live our full lives.

As circumstances come into your life, instead of immediately going into fear, choose instead to turn on a flashlight of curiosity and recognize they are offering you a gift or lesson. If you are willing to shine that light of awareness and use your noticing skills, you will be able to transform your circumstances into opportunities. To do so, you first need to notice your thoughts on the circumstances, pause before making a judgment on them, ask what are some possible benefits or opportunities they may bring, and be willing to ask new and empowered questions. By choosing to face circumstances with empowered thinking, you will gain mastery over the course your life takes from this point forward. You are the person building your exclamation point life.

CHAPTER 3

SETTING YOURSELF FREE

> "When you look into the mirror, what do you see? Do you see the real you, or what you have been conditioned to believe is you? The two are so, so different. One is an infinite consciousness capable of being and creating whatever I choose, the other is an illusion imprisoned by its own perceived and programmed limitations."
>
> — David Icke

In the last chapter, you learned how you can transform your circumstances into opportunities. In this chapter, you will learn how to recognize what beliefs may be holding you back from the results you want to achieve. You will also learn what you can do to repattern those beliefs so you can set yourself free from the hold they have had on you.

RECOGNIZING WHAT'S HOLDING YOU BACK

I had a dream some years ago in which I was imprisoned—almost like a slave, but it was behind bars. I don't remember the other people involved, just my own thinking process. My work was in a laundry room, and when I would look out of this very small window with bars, I could see children laughing and playing. All I could think about was, *How can I escape?* Even if I could cut through the bars, the window was too small for me to climb through.

Every thought in this dream was about my struggle to free myself. It was the same pattern, day after day. The guards would pick me up from my cell, I would work in the laundry room, and then I would be led back to my cell.

It wasn't until the end of my dream when I went to the door of my cell that I realized the cell door had never been locked. I had been holding myself captive the entire time.

How often do we hold ourselves captive through beliefs that limit who we truly are and who we are truly capable of becoming?

We all grew up with others teaching us things to help us navigate our lives. Some were very good things, like, "Look both ways before you cross the street." That one has saved my life multiple times.

But then we were taught other sayings like:

- "Money doesn't grow on trees."
- "All good things must come to an end."
- "Better safe than sorry."
- "A woman's place is in the home."
- "Business before pleasure."
- "Clothes make the man."
- "Don't rock the boat."

- "Money is the root of all evil."
- "Seeing is believing."
- "What goes up must come down."
- "You can't have your cake and eat it too."
- "The rich get richer and the poor get poorer."
- "What will the neighbors think?"
- "Good things come to those who wait."
- "The early bird gets the worm."

(You can easily see how people become indecisive with these last two.)

Many of us just accepted these sayings as truths without thinking twice about them.

However, my mother made me question one of those sayings. As a piano teacher, she was quick to point out, "Practice makes perfect" was not correct. She told me that if I kept practicing and making the same mistake repeatedly, I would never get better; I would only be good at the mistake. She changed the phrase to "Perfect practice makes perfect." She recognized that to get better at anything, you must keep striving for a higher level of what you are trying to attain. To do so, you need to study under someone who is accomplished in what you want to learn. Someone who can teach you techniques you can duplicate in practice.

Here's a list of trained responses it may be worth pushing the internal pause button on to reevaluate:

- "I am not smart enough."
- "I am not pretty enough."
- "I'm too old."

- "I'm too young."
- "Everyone in my family is bad at math."
- "I come from a family where everyone is overweight—it's in our genes."
- "You can only get money through hard work."
- "If I'm successful, then friends and family won't love me anymore."

Remember, the internal pause button lets you notice what you're noticing. Does the statement create an expansive feeling or is it constrictive? What different choice could you make in what you are noticing to create a positive outcome? When in doubt, ask the question, "What would I love?"

EXERCISE

What are some beliefs that have held you back?

_____

_____

_____

Take a second look at those beliefs. How could you change those belief statements into something empowering?

_____

_____

_____

FINDING YOUR BARRIERS

In the book *A Course in Miracles*, a publication from the Foundation for Inner Peace, it says, "Your task is not to seek for love, but merely to seek and find all of the barriers within yourself that you have built against it." In other words, we can seek for what we want outside of us, be that love, a great job, wealth, better health, etc. When we wonder why we can't seem to attain what we are looking for, it is because we keep looking outside ourselves. The truth is we live in a completely abundant universe. If we are not getting the results we want, it isn't because it is not possible for us; it is because we have yet to recognize the barriers we have built up within us that hold us back from having what we want. Finding and repatterning the barriers will set us free.

For example, if you grew up believing "Money is the root of all evil" and money seems to flow in, then out of your hands quickly, and you can't seem to save money, then a barrier in your thinking is stopping you from being able to hold on to money. Your mind equates saving money with being evil, so it does what it can to protect you from being evil. When in this situation, we might tell ourselves, "There is just not enough money to go around." This is how we rationalize why we do not have money. Meanwhile, the barrier we have around money has just gotten stronger.

However, if we remember that we live in a fully abundant universe, then we can ask ourselves, "What in my thinking is creating a barrier to me being able to receive and save money?" You can then start listing what those barriers might be and repattern your thinking around them.

You might first come up with "Money is the root of all evil." Then other statements might fall into place like, "Money doesn't grow on trees," and "There just isn't enough to go around." If you start with "Money is the root of all evil" and question it, your attitude will start shifting as you look at it from a different vantage point.

Here's an example of repatterning "Money is the root of all evil." Think of all the good things money does, such as: Many great things have been accomplished in charities with people giving money—that is a blessing to many, not evil. Money is a helpful currency because it allows me to give when others are in need. Money gives me the means to put a roof over my family's heads and keep us all clothed and fed; this is a blessing to all of us. When I save money, I am able to have more choices in my future—better quality food, a better house, a better car, the opportunity to take my family on vacation, and the freedom to take time off work so I can help a friend in need. These are loving ways I choose to work with money.

From this example, you can see that money no longer looks evil when you look at what it does to support you and those around you.

As you review each barrier, you may have others come up. Write them down so you can repattern them next. As you find the barriers and then repattern them, you will clear up the block that stands between you and what you are desiring to create. What you are seeking is never outside of you. You have the power within you to discover the barriers and repattern them so you can truly set yourself free from the beliefs holding you back from living your exclamation point life.

EXERCISE

In what areas of your life are you currently not having the levels of success you desire?

_____

_____

_____

What are some barriers or beliefs standing in the way of what you would like to be more successful with?

_____

_____

_____

What does repatterning that barrier or belief look like after you have changed your vantage point?

_____

_____

_____

STEPPING OUTSIDE YOUR BOUNDARIES

I have a dear friend, whom I met through quilting. One day, we went on a day trip to get out of town and see some fabric shops in the Chicago suburbs.

While in the western suburbs of Chicago, I mentioned downtown Chicago. She quickly told me she could not drive in Chicago. When I asked her why, she said she had been told by everyone around her that she was unable to drive in downtown Chicago, and she chose to believe them. Since I had lived in several major cities in the United States, I found this amazing. I told her that driving in the city is the same as anywhere else; you just have more cars so you need to pay attention. The driving laws are the same whether you are in a small town or a big city. I then asked her, "Would you like to drive in downtown Chicago?" I let her know I thought she was perfectly capable of driving there if she wanted. I then offered her the backup plan of having me drive in the city if she did not feel she could.

Suddenly, she was like a kid in a candy store—full of enthusiasm and excitement, yet nervous to be stepping outside the boundaries she had accepted from others. "Yes, let's go to downtown Chicago," she said, enlivened by this new opportunity.

So off we went. She became giddy as we got onto highways she had never allowed herself to drive on. A brand-new confidence emerged as she realized driving downtown wasn't nearly as difficult as she had been led to believe. By the time she got into the bumper-to-bumper downtown traffic, she was laughing, waving, and greeting everyone we drove by. Repeatedly, she would say between excited laughs, "I'm doing this!" Yes, she was, and she was doing it on her own terms. Not once did she even feel like she had to ask me to drive for her.

All it took for my friend to change this longstanding boundary was to have someone who believed she could. It gave her a new perspective so she could give herself permission to set herself free.

EXERCISE

What is a boundary you have allowed yourself to have that you would like to move beyond?

_____
_____
_____

Ask yourself, "But what if I could and what if it was easy?" What would you do?

_____
_____
_____

What step can you take today to help you step outside one of your boundaries?

_____
_____
_____

MOVING BEYOND YOUR COMFORT ZONE

Olly Hermon-Taylor, a health and fitness adventurer, coach, and writer, once wrote:

> You'd be forgiven for thinking that the safe, warm, familiar surroundings of your comfort zone are a good thing and where you want to be…. Instead of being a good thing, living life in your comfort zone is incredibly dangerous. It's a place of stagnation and slow death. The graveyard of dreams…. Please don't let another minute pass where you cover your light and hide the gifts you've been given from yourself and the rest of the world.

Hermon-Taylor is right. One's comfort zone robs you of the precious gift of truly having a fulfilling life. When you choose to keep your life in the status quo of your comfort zone, possibilities in your life begin diminishing. As Hermon-Taylor said, it becomes the "graveyard of dreams." Our world was created to grow and evolve continually. When we are not moving forward, we are disempowering ourselves from becoming the fuller and expanded versions of who we came here to be. Every cell in our being is continually evolving and changing. If we are not growing, then the lure of the comfort zone is not only holding us back from growth; it is keeping us from living the best possible version of who we came here to be. You are the only person who will ever be on the planet with the gifts you have waiting within you. You are the only one who can nurture those gifts and share them with all those who are waiting to receive them. If you do not express them and bring them forward in this life, they will be lost forever.

Another example of this truth comes from James C. Collins' book, *Good to Great*. Collins states:

> Good is the enemy of great and that is one of the key reasons why we have so little that becomes great. We don't have great schools, principally because we have good schools. We don't have great government, principally because we have good government. Few people attain great lives, in large part because it is just so easy to settle for a good life.

Settling or staying in one's comfort zone can hold us back from living an exclamation point life. Yes, we need time to rest and reflect, but settling for something less than who we are capable of being is a different thing. When we find ourselves in this position and notice what we are noticing, we can stop and look at ourselves. "Okay, this may be good, but what would great be like?" Allow yourself to dream about great because it is where you will begin living your exclamation point life.

EXERCISE

What are some areas in your life where you are in your comfort zone or have settled?

_____

_____

_____

In those areas of your life, what would great look like?

_____

_____

_____

What can you do today that would bring more great into your life?

_____

_____

_____

LIMITING THOUGHTS ON THE PROWL

Our limiting thoughts that keep us in our comfort zone can be very sneaky. They slither in when we are not looking. This is where "notice what you're noticing" becomes one of your best allies.

I once attended a conference where I shared a hotel room with a friend. I was there the day before my friend arrived, so I picked up the key to the room. One of the first things I noticed was the smell of chlorine in my room from the swimming pool. I dismissed it because the pool was outside my room. My experience with the bed was horrible. It had a lump in the middle, so I kept rolling to the edge of the bed all night. I came very close to falling out of the bed several times that night.

The next night, my friend arrived. I forewarned her about my experience with my bed and hoped her bed would be better. When she laid down on her bed, she said she was having the same experience. We started joking about all kinds of things being stuffed under the mattress.

That night I developed a new strategy for sleeping. I tried to sleep on the "mountaintop" in my bed and started having a little more success. But my roommate ended up falling out of bed; at least the wall caught her before falling on the floor. This drama happened night after night as we laughed about the situation.

After four nights of sleeping in poor conditions, I had an epiphany while in the shower. My "notice what you're noticing" popped into action. "What part of me thinks I should settle for substandard conditions in a high-end hotel where I am paying good money?" With that, the limiting beliefs emerged: "You don't want to create any waves." "It is better for you to have people think you are nice than offend them." "This is why it is better to stay home than travel; you just never know what you are going to get."

As these beliefs and more emerged, I came out of the bathroom dumbfounded with my new awareness. I was now wide awake and excitedly said to my roommate, "I cannot believe it has taken me four days to notice what part of me thinks I should settle for a bad bed in a good hotel?" That statement woke her up from her amnesia about our room as well since she realized she had settled for three days.

I then told her, "I know we only have one night left here, but I want to find out if this hotel has any better beds to sleep on." She agreed.

My initial attempt to speak with the front desk did not go well because part of me remained constricted in my thinking and agitated that I had slept four nights in a bad bed. My conversation with the clerk was met with resistance. She told me, "We change our mattresses every two years and all mattresses in the hotel are the same." I recognized her attitude matched my level of agitation. I knew if I wanted a different outcome, I needed to change my constrictive thinking into expansive thinking by dreaming what kind of experience I would *love* to have for my last night's stay at the hotel. This was my opportunity to move out of circumstance thinking into creating an experience I would love by design.

After taking the time to envision my desired outcome, I went back to the front desk empowered by my vision and with an expanded vantage point. As I was standing in line, I looked at the four people behind the service counter and asked inwardly, "Which person can help me realize my dream of a good night's sleep in a comfortable bed?" I had a knowingness it would be the last person at the far end of the counter. Her station opened for the person in front of me in line. With that, the person in front of me, who had been waiting for ten minutes with me, said, "Why don't you go ahead? I think I'm going to wait for someone else." I was grateful.

When I got to the counter, I said, "I wonder whether you could help me have a different experience in your hotel than what I have had the past four nights?" My question opened the door to a positive outcome. My roommate and I got to spend our last night in a larger room, without the smell of chlorine, and with comfortable beds. I had been successful in catching my limiting thoughts and repatterning them for an empowered outcome.

EXERCISE

Is there an area in your life where you can see some limiting thoughts have come to visit?

_____

_____

_____

_____

_____

What steps can you take today to repattern them so you can move forward empowered?

_____

_____

_____

SUMMARY

To set yourself free from the limiting beliefs that have kept you from fulfilling the results you desire, you first need to begin recognizing the thoughts holding you back. Are they beliefs you learned from other people, or ones you have carried from your own past experiences? Once you discover what is holding you back, what can you do to repattern those beliefs so they can now serve you in building a more vibrant life? As Smokey the Bear says, "Only you can prevent forest fires." You are the only one who can stop entertaining the limiting thoughts and repattern them with supportive thinking.

To move forward from here, you will need to begin stepping outside of your former boundaries and moving beyond your comfort zone. Once you do, you will discover how freeing and liberating this new way of living your life can be.

Just remember, those old limiting thoughts are just waiting to sneak back in. They are well-worn ruts on the road of your life. But if you keep noticing them and repatterning them when they arrive, you will continue to build new and better pathways to lead you to your exclamation point life.

CHAPTER 4

—⚛—

DISCOVERING WHAT IS EMERGING IN YOU

"Learn to get in touch with the silence within yourself, and know that everything in life has purpose. There are no mistakes, no coincidences, all events are blessings given to us to learn from."

— Elisabeth Kübler-Ross

In the last chapter, we discussed setting yourself free by recognizing what is holding you back and repatterning your barriers. You learned to step outside of your boundaries and move beyond your comfort zone to create a vibrant life. In this chapter, you will discover how the infinite side of your nature, which is Infinite Intelligence working through us, wants to be expressed in this world. That infinite side can often be found in what you are passionate about or what you are longing for.

RECOGNIZING THE GREATER SIDE OF YOU

In a meditation series Oprah Winfrey and Deepak Chopra created on

"Becoming What You Believe," Oprah states in the Day Two meditation:

> When I was a young girl growing up in the church, I actually believed I was God's child, and kind of thought Jesus was my brother. I just never doubted my belief.... Because I believed I was a child of God, I did believe anything was possible. Those beliefs shaped my reality. I didn't know what that reality would lead to, but I knew who I was before I could even articulate it, and that has led me to the life I live today.

Oprah's personal story gives us the opportunity to look way back to where we started. Was there a place in your life where you felt deeply connected and knew there was something greater than your circumstances?

As a little girl, I just loved singing. When I sang, my whole world was brighter. Singing was magical and connected me to something greater than I was on my own. It's as if when I sang, peace, joy, and love came to visit me and filled every corner of my being. This was my first conscious awareness of being connected to something greater than myself, and it seemed to be radiating from within.

Pema Chödrön, a Tibetan Buddhist nun, wrote in her book, *No Time to Lose*, "Our true nature is like a precious jewel: although it may be temporarily buried in mud, it remains completely brilliant and unaffected. We simply have to uncover it."

Each of us has a gift that lies within our true nature. This is the divine spark of God within us. No one is without this gift, no matter what has happened in his or her life. It may be covered and hidden from view, but that doesn't mean it is not present and waiting for you to discover it. It is the very part of you that wants to be discovered so that as it comes forth in your life, you can begin living the life you came to live.

EXERCISE

In what ways can you nurture that part of you that is beginning to recognize the "precious jewel" inside of you?

_____

_____

_____

In what ways do you connect to your true nature, that divine spark of God within you?

_____

_____

_____

LEARNING FROM CABBAGE BUTTERFLIES

For much of my life, my family would summer vacation in northern Minnesota on the Canadian border. We loved going to the northwoods to boat, fish, and be in awe of nature.

One summer, we were there at the most amazing time because we had the opportunity to experience the migration of the cabbage butterflies. We would see them come from the north side of our cabin, stop at the flowers to gain some nourishment, and then make their journey across the lake. There were millions of these little white butterflies. They reminded me of watching the cherry blossoms when the wind blows in Washington, DC, except they didn't fall. Their delicate wings were creating a beautiful ballet across the vast expanse of water.

My dad and I took the opportunity to sit on a bench near the lake to marvel over the butterflies' migration. I said to my dad, "Isn't it amazing that in their little bodies they know where they're supposed to go. It is like a beacon calling them home." My dad replied, "We are very much like the butterflies. God has imprinted in us that same sort of inner drive calling us forward. If we listen, we will know the direction of the path, but then it is up to us to follow."

The butterflies had a long, long journey to fly, but they knew where to go and they followed it. As I watched them fly across the lake, I was amazed by their strength because they had a long way to go before they could land again.

God has that plan for you as well, and it has been imprinted in your heart as your longing, as something that impassions and inspires you. Listen to it, and follow it with every beat of your heart; then you will create the most amazing life. Like the butterfly, it will take strength, rest, nourishment, and time for you to complete the journey.

EXERCISE

What are some things you are passionate about now or were passionate about when you were younger?

_____

_____

_____

What longing or passion is calling you forth at this point in your life?

_____

_____

_____

LOOKING AT YOUR LIFE IN A NEW WAY

Genevieve Behrend was the only student who got to study mental science with Thomas Troward, whose works influenced the New Thought movement and mystic Christianity. In her book *Your Invisible Power*, Behrend states: "So be yourself and enjoy Life in your own Divine way. Do not fear to be your true self, for everything you want, wants you."

When I read this passage, something woke within me. It was as if I had discovered a missing link in my life. I have since come to realize we are all connected to the Infinite Intelligence of the Universe. God has planted a seed in each of us for us to discover and bring forth into the world. We can recognize the seed because it is what we are passionate about. Some refer to this seed as your purpose. Once we discover it and take action to become our "true self," we will draw to us the experiences needed to fulfill our purpose, "for everything you want, wants you."

If we can just be who we came here to be and connect with our true nature, we will not only have joy, but we will discover that everything we want and desire has been waiting for us to find it.

Emmet Fox, an early twentieth century New Thought spiritual

leader and author, wrote the book *Make Your Life Worthwhile*. In this book, Fox wrote, "When you really desire to be or to do something…it is a sign that God wants you to do that and above all…that God who gave you the wish will give you the accomplishment too." Fox understood that God wants us to discover and connect to what we are truly meant to bring forth in this life. This is God's thought finding expression through us, and it is not separate from us. Instead, we are co-creating together. When we follow our passion, we are fulfilling God's expression in this world. By doing so, he supports us 100 percent by helping our dream come to fruition.

The Brazilian novelist Paulo Coelho states this a little differently in his acclaimed book *The Alchemist*: "When you want something, all the universe conspires in helping to achieve it." Coelho, like Genevieve Behrend and Emmet Fox, is revealing that when we move in the direction of our desire and passion, the Universe will collaborate with us by bringing us what we need to achieve our desire. We are coworkers with the Universe, and as we choose to build our passion into a dream, God will be there to light our path and provide us with the opportunities to succeed.

EXERCISE

What are some experiences you have had where you knew that what you wanted, wanted you?

_____

_____

_____

_____

What steps can you take today to move forward in an area of your life you are passionate about?

_____

_____

_____

How does knowing that God supports your dream 100 percent help you take a leap of faith in building your vision?

_____

_____

_____

WINNING ATTITUDE

It was the middle of the night, and I was not sleeping well. I had allowed too much to be weighing on my mind. My stomach was upset, so I thought it best to sit up for a while. When I decided to go on Facebook, I saw a Nametest a friend had posted. It was titled, "What name would God give you?"

I thought, "I am definitely open to learning what name God has to give me," so I logged in to find out my results.

It said, "Anne – the Winner. You are always in God's thoughts, Anne! His name for you is the Winner. This name perfectly suits you because it describes your true core. In the Bible, God promised you: 'Do not fear for I have redeemed you; I have summoned you by name; You are mine.'"

When I read this, I was so glad that God's name for me was "winner" and not "whiner"! I then stepped back a moment and asked myself, "Where have I been placing my energy? Am I being the winner that God summoned me to be by name, or am I whining about circumstances in my life?"

Sometimes we forget that we were born winners. The Bible says that God created us in his image, so how could we be anything but winners?

I'm familiar with a healing technique that helps people release strong emotions they have been holding onto that are limiting them. As I recall, at the end of the clearing work, the practitioner's notes say, "Remind the client that they are the product of the great sperm race. They have been a winner from the very start!" This made me laugh when I heard it, but at the same time, how true.

We are winners, from the beginning to the end of our lives. Sometimes we simply forget and can fall into being a whiner instead of a winner.

It's time to remember who you were born to be—a winner!

EXERCISE

What does it feel like to be a winner in your own life?

_____

_____

_____

How does knowing you have always been and will always be a winner change your perspective on circumstances?

_____

_____

_____

What does the winner in you want to accomplish today?

_____

_____

_____

CLAIMING YOUR INHERITANCE

My father was an ordained minister in the Lutheran Church. During most of my childhood, he served the larger church body instead of a parish, so it was extra special for me when I got to hear him preach a sermon.

I remember my father telling a story in one of his sermons about a young boy who had been born out of wedlock. When he and his mom moved to another town, everywhere he went, people would ask him "Who's your daddy?" He was mocked and ridiculed so often that he became ashamed of who he was.

This boy loved going to the church, but he would often show up and hide in the back so no one would know he was there. One day as church ended, he got stuck in the crowd and did not get to sneak out before the new minister caught up with him.

The minister said, "Now you're the son of…." A hush came over the room and the little boy so wanted to run away. The minister, recognizing the shift in the room, said to the little boy, "Now you are the son of God—go out and claim your inheritance!"

What the minister said shifted everything for that little boy. He now saw himself as a child of God and claimed it as his inheritance. This shift changed the course of his life from that point forward, and eventually, that little boy became the governor of Tennessee.

We are all children of God, part of the Infinite Universe, and the inheritance is ours. It is simply up to us to claim it. We were winners before we were born; we simply must let go of our limiting thoughts and harness the winner we already are!

EXERCISE

What gifts has God given you in your inheritance?

_____

_____

_____

If you believed that everything you dreamed could be possible, how might that change your current reality?

_____

_____

_____

SUMMARY

In discovering what is emerging in you, first recognize that you are more than your thoughts, circumstances, and physical body. Something greater within you is calling you forth to live your greater potential.

That something greater in you is calling you like a beacon—ever-present and driving you forward. The cabbage butterfly is willing to fly thousands of miles during its migration. Because the pull to fly where it is supposed to go is so strong, the butterfly is willing to do whatever necessary to complete the journey.

For us, the beacon shows up as a longing or passion that keeps calling us until we answer. The Universe is ever working with us as we listen to the deeper call within us. It is a co-creative experience. What we want, wants us. When you choose to connect with the infinite side of your nature, new doorways of possibility will emerge for you, and you will begin down your path to creating your exclamation point life.

CHAPTER 5

DARING TO DREAM BY DEFINING WHAT YOU WANT

> "You have to leave the city of your comfort and go into the wilderness of your intuition. What you'll discover will be wonderful. What you'll discover is yourself."
>
> — Alan Alda

In the last chapter, you discovered that what is emerging in you—what you are passionate about or what you are longing for—wants to be expressed in this world. In this chapter, you will have the opportunity to take a deeper dive by daring to dream and really define what you want.

DREAMING OF A NEW CAR

Let me share with you a story about how to create a vision of what you want even when circumstances tell you that you can't. This story focuses on a smaller goal than a life vision, but it shows what is possible when you dare to dream by defining what you want in detail.

My old car was developing some bad problems. I could not turn on the ventilation system without breathing in exhaust fumes. That meant I had to drive in the winter with a blanket on, and in the summer, I had to have all my windows open and pray I didn't get heatstroke. At this time in my life, I was trying to recover from chronic fatigue syndrome, so I did not have much money in the bank, let alone money to buy a car. Knowing my car was in bad condition and my financial situation wasn't good enough to get a better car was a tough circumstance to be in.

My parents said, "Anne, you need to get a new car." I would respond with all the reasons I couldn't afford a new car. But then a thought occurred to me: "If I could get a car, what would it be?" That simple thought propelled me out of circumstance-based thinking into dreaming.

I bought a book on cars and started researching what would be the best car for my desires. Then I started going to car lots and test-driving them. If they didn't have a comfortable seat, I checked them off my list. I got the car narrowed down to a Ford Contour. I wanted my car to have a V6 engine, be the color Pacific Green Clearcoat, and have a gray interior. (In other words, I wanted my car to have a silver lining.)

I was so passionate about what I wanted that my two sisters went out and bought Contours before me! They figured I had done the research and knew what I was talking about.

My issue was that it was coming to the end of the car-year season. V6 car engines were hard to find, let alone a Pacific Green Clearcoat, and in this model year, I had only seen tan interiors, not the silver lining I was looking for. This was circumstance-based thinking.

DARING TO DREAM BY DEFINING WHAT YOU WANT

In the meantime, I continued to dream, even though I had no idea how I would pay for my new car. I just had to put the "how" on hold. I cut out a picture of the car I wanted and I wrote down on my calendar which day I was going to buy it. I contacted people across the country who might be able to help me find the car.

Then someone who knew I was financially just getting back on my feet chose to help me by giving me money for a down payment. I cried as my heart filled with gratitude. The "how" had been answered in a way I could not have expected.

However, the night before the date I had put on my calendar, I still had not found the car I was looking for, so I was feeling doubtful. I decided to go to the Ford dealer closest to my house to test drive a 4-cylinder car one more time. I was almost ready to toss in the towel and let the dream go.

I got there just before closing time. When the salesman met me, I said I was there to look at the 4-cylinder Contours he had on the lot, adding, "Although I am looking at the 4-cylinder, I really want a V6."

The next words out of his mouth were, "We just brought a V6 into the showroom this afternoon. I don't know what you think about the color green."

I could barely breathe as I tried not to look too excited. I replied, "Yeah, green is okay."

When he took me into the showroom, there was the V6 Contour—not in Hunter Green, but in the Pacific Green Clearcoat of my dream. The interior color was the silver lining I had dreamed of. I would recognize two surprise additions to that car as gifts. First, it was the model SE, which to me meant "spiritual exercise," and second, it was equipped with a spoiler on the back. It was time for me to learn how to spoil myself.

The salesman let me take the car home for the evening to think about it. The next day, with the assistance of a friend who was a car salesman, he helped me get the price lowered on the car. When I signed the financial papers and saw the loan payments, it was exactly what I was able to afford.

What had just happened? I had just bought a car that circumstance thinking would have told me was impossible. By creating a very clear vision of what I wanted, I was able to buy this car on the precise date I had written in my vision and have payments I could afford. I got exactly what I had dreamed of with something better still—my new Contour V6 in Pacific Green Clearcoat with the silver lining. I was completely in awe of what had just transpired in my life and grateful to God for the incredible blessing.

This type of experience can happen to you if you dare to dream beyond circumstances that tell you what you want cannot be done. Allow yourself the opportunity to say to yourself, "But if I could have this dream, what would it look like?" Several other key factors are also necessary in creating your dream—being passionate about it, defining its details, having gratitude throughout the process, trusting that it is all working out, and eating, breathing, and living your dream as if it is already yours—keeping an open hand to God for this or something better.

EXERCISE

What dream is waking up in you?

_____

_____

_____

Are you passionate about it? How does it make you feel?

_____

_____

_____

Define your current dream in more detail:

_____

_____

_____

Is this dream worth your time and energy to create?

_____

_____

_____

CREATING YOUR VISION

Mark Twain, the American writer and humorist, once said, "I can teach anybody how to get what they want out of life. The problem is that I can't find anybody who can tell me what they want." When I first read this quote, I laughed, but as I thought about it, I realized Mark Twain knew what he was talking about. So many people are so busy living their day-to-day lives that they have not taken the time to step back and ask, "What do I want?" To live your best life, you will first need to define what you want.

If I asked you what you do and how you do it, you could probably give me a quick answer. If I asked you why you do what you do, you might have to think about it. If I asked you whether it was what you truly wanted to do with the precious time in your life, what would your answer be, and how long would you have to think about it?

We get so programmed by the routines we create in our lives that we forget a key ingredient. In creating your exclamation point life, the passion behind your desires is what drives you and gives you the reason behind why you do what you do. If you start with what you are passionate about and have that lead you forward, your life will begin to have more meaning and will grow in leaps and bounds.

If you could truly live the life you would love, what would it look like? What are you passionate about? It's not about creating a vision of what you think you can have. It is about creating a vision that is limitless, with nothing being held back. This means letting go of the "I can't have this because I am _____ (too fat, too old, too young, too tall, too short, too poor, etc.)."

If you could live your most vibrant life and time and money were not a factor, what would it look like? Would you desire to have more optimal health? Where would you live, near the ocean or in a big city? Or would you prefer living in a rural setting or in the mountains? Would you be sharing your life with a special loved one? Would you have family or friends living with you or nearby? What would you be doing to share your gifts with the world? What kind of work or volunteer work would you do to fill your heart and soul? Would you take vacations? If so, where would you love to travel? And so on….

Ask yourself these questions and any others that come to mind. Search with your deepest yearnings for the answers. This exercise, if done repeatedly, will help you develop your vision, and in time, you will find that your answers will keep expanding and new horizons will begin to emerge in your vision that perhaps you never allowed yourself to dream of before. By working with my vision over time, it has grown and expanded in ways I never could have imagined. So, dare to dream and dream boldly. Create a vibrant vision of what you would love. Simply leave behind the "I'm too _____ for that" and put the "How could that happen?" on hold.

EXERCISE

Based on the above questions, what would you love to create in your life?

_____

_____

_____   _____

_____

List five things you would do if time, money, age, and circumstance were not an issue for you:

1. _____

2. _____

3. _____

4. _____

5. _____

BE CAREFUL WHAT YOU ASK FOR

We have all heard the saying, "Be careful what you ask for; you might just get it." In creating your vision, it is very important to be specific about the details.

I have a friend who is a nurse. She had always dreamed of getting a Harley by the time she was forty. Just before her fortieth birthday, she got a patient named "Harley." We both laughed about it at the time, but she did get what she had asked for.

Just imagine if she had been clearer with the universe about wanting a new 2000 Harley-Davidson XL Sportster 883 Custom motorcycle in Real Teal Pearl? She simply had not thought it out in that detail, nor had she written it down or taken any action steps to help create it. It had simply remained a wish.

As important as being specific is, the importance of adding the statement at the end "This or something better" is equally important. As you are creating your vision, it is important to treat it with an open hand. You want to let the Universe bring the best version to you; after all, God can see the bigger picture, while sometimes, we have our blinders on. Don't be attached to your vision showing up exactly as you envisioned; be open to it being grander than you could have ever imagined.

EXERCISE

When have there been times when you could have been more specific about what you wanted to receive different results?

_____

_____

Where can you be more specific with your current dream so you create better results?

_____

_____

_____

CREATING WITH YOUR THOUGHTS

Wallace D. Wattles, an early twentieth century American New Thought author, wrote the book *The Science of Getting Rich*. In it, Wallace wrote:

> There is a thinking Stuff from which all things are made, and which, in its original state, permeates, penetrates, and fills the interspaces of the universe. A thought, in this Substance, produces

the thing that is imaged by the thought. Man can form things in his thought, and by impressing his thought upon Formless Substance, can cause the thing he thinks about to be created.

After I read this, I understood why I had found the car I had dreamt about. It was not just a gift from God. It was the product of me working with God in the "Formless Substance" of the universe. I first had to imagine the thought for it to be created.

When we become co-creators with this "Formless Substance," any and all things are possible. The more passionate we are about our thoughts, the more we will impress them upon that Formless Substance so it can create what is imagined by the thought. We cannot achieve what we want by thinking it just once. We must own the thought, live it with passion, and understand that the thought is already becoming reality. This is a co-creative process. First, you think the thought and hold steady the image of your true desire. Then have full trust that what you are dreaming is being created.

Note that if you have any negative thoughts you are passionate about, they will be created in the Formless Substance as well. It is, therefore, important to practice noticing what you're noticing to help you transform those negative thoughts more quickly so you don't create more of what you don't want.

And most importantly, you want to have gratitude and not be attached to how what you want comes to you. When creating your vision, have gratitude that this gift of creation is yours, and at the end of describing what you want, state, "This or something better." That way, the universe is not limited in how it brings you the gift of your dream.

For example, my Ford Contour came with something even better than I imagined. God wanted me to know I was worth spoiling by having the spoiler on the back, and the model SE taught me this was a spiritual exercise to learn how to manifest my dreams. God has a sense of humor and will bring you wonderful delights and surprises when you are open to the possibilities of "This or something better" for your vision.

EXERCISE

List a time when you were passionate about something you wanted and it came true for you:

_____

_____

What did you learn from that experience that you can apply to your current dream?

_____

_____

ORDERING WHAT YOU WANT FROM LIFE

How do you order what you want from life? It is much like ordering a pizza.

If you want to order a pizza, you call a pizza parlor. The person who answers the phone asks you what you want.

If you say, "I just want a pizza," the person at the pizza place is going to say, "What kind of pizza?" And, if you say, "Just a pizza will do," what do you think will happen? You may end up with a sauerkraut and anchovy personal-sized pizza waiting for pickup, when you really wanted a large supreme pizza delivered to your door.

After an hour, you call the pizza place and say, "Where is my pizza?" and the person on the phone says, "It has been waiting for you to pick up for the last forty minutes." When you pick up the pizza, you discover it is the worst version of a pizza you can imagine, and it is also cold, and you wonder why life is treating you so badly.

On the other hand, if you call to order a pizza and tell the person who answers the phone, "I would like a large supreme pizza, thin crust with extra sauce and hold the olives, for delivery," what do you think you will get? When that pizza arrives, you will be thrilled that you got what you wanted.

Just like it is for ordering pizza, it is the same for everything else you can dream of for your life. For the Universe to help you with your dream, you need to be as specific as you can. Without specificity, the Universe cannot deliver to you what you truly want, and then you become disenchanted that life doesn't give you what you hoped for.

To help you develop more details for your dream, start by writing down as many details as you can about the vision you hold for your life. It is okay if up until now you have not allowed yourself to dream about much or you have forgotten how to dream. This is the time to roll up your sleeves, jump in with both feet, and truly dare to dream. If age, time, health, and money are not issues for you and you can truly have what you want, then: What kind of health do you envision? How would you love to express your gifts in the world—through your life's work or volunteering? What kind of relationships do you dream of? What would you do with time and money freedom? When you have finished answering these questions, write at the end, "This or something better." This allows the universe to give you even something better than you imagined.

Dare to dream and dream big as you imagine your life. Who are you as that person in your vision? Write as much as you can down on paper, for you are much more likely to create the vision you imagined by writing it down.

EXERCISE

This exercise is an opportunity to write your vision in greater detail—act as if anything is possible; there are no limits. If you can dream it, you can create it. What would you love? What does your health look like? How are your relationships? What does your vocation or how you express yourself to the world look like? What do you like doing with your time and financial freedom?

_____

_____

_____

_____

_____

_____

_____

SUMMARY

As you begin to define your vision and what you want to create in your life, remember to be bold and dream a big, bright, and beautiful future for yourself. The dream that is calling you asks you to stretch beyond the previous boundaries you have set for yourself. If you know how to make your dream happen, your vision is not expansive enough; it is only a nice goal. You need to dare to reach higher, to the places that are limitless in their capacities to move and transform your life in ways you have yet to imagine.

When I dreamt of a new car, I was specific about what I wanted. Even though I did not know how, I put that thought on hold and played full out with creating my vision. By leaving an open hand to the results, I ended up with more than I had asked for.

The more specific you are with clarifying your dream on paper, the better quality your results will be. Once you have created a clear vision, remember to have gratitude that your vision is coming into your life and to keep an open hand with your vision of "This or something better." These statements keep you in alignment and help take limits off the Universe in creating with you the best possible outcome for your dream and everyone involved in it.

CHAPTER 6

TRYING YOUR DREAM ON FOR SIZE

"If you can dream it, you can do it."
— Tom Fitzgerald, Walt Disney Imagineer

In the last chapter, you discovered how to take a deeper dive by daring to dream and really define what you want. In this chapter, you will have the opportunity to try your dream on for size and see whether it is worthy of you.

LEARNING FROM GLASS SLIPPERS

Some of the best things we can learn about life are hidden away in fairy tales. In this land of make believe, we can try on the different parts of our dream. Through our own daydreams and childhood fairytales, the doorway of imagination opens for us.

As children, many of us fell in love with the fairy tale "Cinderella" because we resonated with parts of the story. Later in life, however, we may have been told, "This kind of thing only happens in fairy tales." However, part of us still believes dreams come true. That part of you is who this chapter is speaking to. Dreams do come true.

So let's go back to Cinderella's story to help move us into trying on our dream. Cinderella, like many of us, comes into this world with her gifts; she is a kind girl and all the animals love her. However, her stepmother and two stepsisters are cruel to her because they are jealous of her charm and beauty. She works all day for them and tries to make them happy, but she can't see her way out of the circumstances. Discontent settles in. She longs for something else, but she feels stuck.

Then one day, an invitation arrives to go to a royal ball. The king is summoning all the eligible young women in the kingdom to the ball so the prince can choose a wife. The invitation represents the awakening of the dream that occurs in each of us. It triggers in us the realization that there is something more to life than just the circumstances we are in. And, just like Cinderella, we start thinking, "What if I could do that?"

With the invitation, possibilities begin to emerge for Cinderella. She allows herself to dream of going to the ball, and she starts with what she has to move in the direction of her dream. In the attic, she finds a dress that belonged to her mother; even though it is outdated, she knows she can transform it. She believes in her dream and is using what she has to reach it. Her stepmother tries to hold her back by giving her a lot of chores. This situation is just like our old belief systems trying to keep us occupied with other things so we will not fulfill our dreams.

Cinderella's dream will not be squashed so easily; the mice and birds work as a team to fix her dress and adorn it with ribbons and beads discarded by the stepsisters until the simple dress is transformed into a splendid gown. Similarly, there are people in your life who will support you in creating your dream. They believe in you even when you have lost hope. Because of the love you have first given them, they will support you in creating your dream.

Unfortunately, the mean stepsisters see Cinderella in the dress and tear it apart. Cinderella's dream of going to the ball is now dashed, so she goes into the garden to cry. This is when her fairy godmother appears. Similarly, circumstances will show up in your life to try to dash your dreams, so your passion for your dream needs to be stronger than any circumstance. When you hold true to your vision, the Universe will support you in creating your dream.

In Cinderella's case, the fairy godmother waves her wand and creates a coach from a pumpkin; she transforms the mice into horses, a rat into a coachman, and lizards into footmen. When she waves her magic wand once more, Cinderella finds herself in a lovely gown with glass slippers. The Universe has fully supported her in creating her dream, but it is up to Cinderella not only to put on and wear her dream, but she must now live her dream to make it come true.

Her fairy godmother warns Cinderella that the spell will be broken by midnight and she will return to her previous life. Cinderella now has the opportunity to try on her dream and wear it. If it is a match, it is going to be up to Cinderella to step into her vision. The Universe can only give us the tools to help us fulfill our dream; the rest is up to us in making it come true.

At the ball, Prince Charming is taken by Cinderella and they dance. What she wants, wants her. She has attracted her dream and is living the life she has imagined as if it is hers, trying the dream on for size.

When midnight comes, Cinderella must leave the ball and go back to her previous life, but something happens as she rushes to leave the ball. One of her glass slippers falls off.

The glass slipper represents her dream. She had just tried on her vision, and it was the vision she wanted to live. By leaving one of her glass slippers behind, she creates a bridge between her life of circumstances and her dream. The glass slipper represents how her dream did not transform back to her old life at the stroke of midnight. The dream is stronger than circumstance at this point because Cinderella has been feeding the dream. One slipper ends up with the prince and the other is with her. She has been changed by her dream, and by creating the bridge from her life of circumstances to the life of her dreams, she will no longer be pulled back to her old life. Trying on her dream solidifies that she wants the dream of marrying the Prince. The pull to the dream is now stronger than any circumstance.

When the Prince comes looking for the maiden whose foot fits in the slipper, the evil stepsisters both push their way in to try on the glass slipper. The stepsisters keep trying and trying to shove their feet into a shoe that does not fit. Cinderella asks whether she might try while the stepsisters taunt her. Circumstances no longer have control of Cinderella. When she tries on the glass slipper of her dream, it fits perfectly.

Of course, then Cinderella marries Prince Charming and they live happily ever after. She becomes one with her vision and lives the life she has dreamed.

As you try on your dream, be mindful to let the dream flow with what you would love and pay attention to whether you are trying to force anything to fit. The glass slipper of your dream will fit you perfectly, and you are the only one your dream will fit.

EXERCISE

If you could create anything you would love in this moment, what would it be?

_____

_____

_____

As you start trying on your dream, what are you noticing about its fit? Pay attention to anything that might need to be tweaked or even discarded.

_____

_____

_____

PLAYING DRESS-UP

When I was a little girl, I loved playing dress-up with my sisters or friends. My mom had some gowns we could dress up in, and we would fumble around as we tried to walk in her high heels. If we snuck into her makeup, we would inevitably have lipstick smeared halfway across our faces. It didn't matter; we were pretending to be whomever we wanted to be.

Maybe we were princesses, or schoolteachers, or doctors. It didn't matter; we were just trying it on. If we got bored with pretending to be one thing, we just said to the other person, "I want to pretend to be something else now." The next thing we knew, we were trying on a different persona, even being an animal, a tree, or something else.

Too often as adults, we forget how important it is to pretend and play dress-up. As children, I believe we often play dress-up to discover more of the world around us, and if we didn't like what we dressed up as, we left that image behind.

As you look at your dream, play with it. Wear it as if it is already yours and allow yourself to experience it with all your senses. What does it look like? Does it fill you with joy? Is there a certain fragrance in the air? Any certain sounds in the scene you are creating? What do the people who are benefiting from your dream say to you? Ask yourself these questions and more. Be specific and pay attention to how your dream feels.

Your vision will change as you play dress-up with your dream. You will start being able to look at parts and say, "That's not quite it, but adding ABC will make it better." The more you try on different versions of your dream, the clearer you will become about what you want your dream to look like. This, in turn, helps strengthen the burning desire for your dream with the parts of you that want to create your exclamation point life. The more you play with your dream by trying on different versions of it, the stronger and more detailed your vision will become and the more joy you will have in watching it unfold.

EXERCISE

Try on your dream. What do you notice about your dream when you try it on?

_____

_____

Are there any areas of your dream that feel constrictive and make you want to try a different version of it? If so, what are some other ideas you can try on to create a better vision?

_____

_____

_____

TESTING YOUR DREAM

In her book *Building Your Field of Dreams*, Mary Manin Morrissey writes about testing your dream with five essential questions:

1. Does this dream enliven me?
2. Does this dream align with my core values?
3. Do I need help from a higher source to make this dream come true?
4. Will this dream require me to grow into more of my true self?
5. Will this dream ultimately bless others?

These questions are significant in helping you to explore your dream at a much deeper level. They allow you to make sure your dream is worthy of you because, after all, you are exchanging your life for it.

This is where you begin to try on your dream. To create an exclamation point life, the vision you hold for yourself must answer a resounding yes to these five questions; otherwise, your dream is not big enough, and it is not worthy of your time and effort. If you cannot answer yes to these questions, you will want to reevaluate your dream.

You want to be passionate about your dream because as you create your vision, at times, you will need to walk through some barriers; your passion will drive you on to the realization of your dreams. Living your exclamation point life will require you to grow in ways you could not have previously imagined, so you need to be willing to embrace the process (including the good, the bad, and the ugly).

At times, you may feel unskilled. Be open to learning, and trust the Universe will support you along the way. And, if ever you get stuck, remember to come back to the questions: What do I want? What would I love?

EXERCISE

Test your dream with the five questions above. Were you able to answer yes to all of them?

1. _____

2. _____

3. _____

4. _____

5. _____

If not, what do you need to consider shifting in your vision to have it be a resounding yes?

___

___

___

BEING OPEN TO UNEXPLORED OPTIONS

If you answer no to any of the five essential questions above, take the time to look at what that means to you.

As I was looking to take my next step in the vision for my life, I had to reevaluate my dream. I had always wanted to go back to school to get my Master's degree in architecture so I could teach architecture at the university. When I applied and was accepted into a graduate program, I was excited that I had the opportunity to fulfill this dream.

An interesting thing happened in the process. I found myself getting hung up on the second question: Does this dream align with my core values? All the other questions had "yes" for an answer. One of my core values is family, and although I had lived far away from family in the past, at that point in my life, I felt it important to live near my parents to assist them with their needs. To follow this dream at that time would have put me a full day's driving away from them, and there was no convenient means of air travel to see them in case of an emergency. I was not okay with being too far away if they needed me.

I then had to reevaluate what I was truly passionate about in the dream. Was it teaching architecture, or was it something else? What I realized once I reevaluated the dream was that the main thing I wanted to do was teach others how to reach for their full potential, no matter what field they were in. I had held on to an old dream of architecture because I had a degree in it. Once I reevaluated my dream and aligned it with my core values, the love for my dream was able to grow and blossom in ways I never could have imagined.

It was important to give myself permission to review my dream when I could not answer yes to one of the questions. I also could not settle for the dream I had created in the past as being the only possibility for me.

EXERCISE

What insights have you gained thus far that can help you strengthen your dream?

_____

_____

If there are parts of your dream you now know you need to change, what would you like to add or subtract to make your dream better?

_____

_____

KEEPING YOUR EYE ON THE DREAM

Once you have tested your dream and you can answer yes to all five of the questions, it's time to start wearing your dream instead of just trying it on. Wearing your vision helps you keep your eye on the dream.

Kris Heap of Successify.net wrote an article, *Walking in Circles?—Six Steps to Define Your Vision*. In the article's conclusion, he writes:

> The people who get ahead and make a difference in life are those who have a plan they are passionate about. They have a vision they feel passionate about and they work every day towards reaching that vision. They have placed the mountain on the horizon to make sure every step they take is a step forward. They can avoid the side paths and diversions on their journey because they can see the straight line toward their goal.

Heap is saying that you must first be passionate about your dream, then take daily action steps in its direction. By doing so, you are always keeping the goal in sight, and you will not get sidetracked by things that do not support your dream. One of the easiest ways to keep your eye on your dream is to put your action steps on a calendar—write down what steps you are going to take and when you are going to complete each step. Even if you only spend five minutes a day working on your dream, each day you will be a step closer to moving into your exclamation point life.

EXERCISE

After trying on your dream, what are some action steps you can take to move your vision forward?

_____

_____

_____

Add those action steps to your calendar.

SUMMARY

Trying on your dream is such an important step in creating your best vision. It's an opportunity just to try things on and see whether they fit. Be mindful of whether you are trying to force something to fit. You want the fit to be just right for you. After all, you are exchanging your current life for your dream, so make sure it's worthy of you.

Take the time to ask good questions of the dream you are considering. Ultimately, make sure you can answer "yes" to the five essential questions with all parts of your vision.

Also, be willing to look at dreams from your past that you may not have fulfilled; you may find some interesting pieces that could help you with the dream you are creating.

Next, start wearing your dream by putting passion into your vision, and take daily action steps to nurture your dream. Keeping your eye on your vision is essential if you are going to bring your dream into fruition; otherwise, distractions will start sneaking in and robbing you of your dream. Remember, the best way you can help yourself is to put your action steps on the calendar and hold yourself accountable to them. This process will help you create the success you desire in building your exclamation point life.

CHAPTER 7

EMBRACING WHAT'S EMERGING IN YOU

"The secret of change is to focus all of your energy, not on fighting the old, but on building the new."

— Socrates

In the last chapter, you discovered what trying on your dream feels like, and you had the opportunity to clarify your vision. In this chapter, you will learn to embrace what's emerging within you as you move into living your vision.

METAMORPHOSING FROM A CATERPILLAR TO A BUTTERFLY

When I was a kid, I was fascinated with butterflies. I had a butterfly net to see whether I could catch them so I could get a closer look at what made them so beautiful. In school when we learned about butterflies, the teacher told us a butterfly was initially a caterpillar. I thought, "How can that be? A butterfly is so beautiful. How could it come from such humble beginnings?"

What an amazing transformation a caterpillar goes through to become a butterfly. I love how nature gives us something to witness to teach us about ourselves.

As a kid, I understood what was a caterpillar and what was a butterfly, but what about the metamorphosis thing caterpillars do to become butterflies? At the time, that was something completely beyond my understanding.

The caterpillar goes through multiple stages before it becomes a butterfly. When it is initially hatched from an egg, it is ravenous and wants to eat everything in sight. As it grows, it eventually outgrows its skin and molts, or lets go of its old skin, so it can grow into its new skin. This doesn't happen just once, but five times. When it has completed its growing cycle as a caterpillar, it is ready for its final molt and big change. It hangs upside-down from a twig and spins a chrysalis around it. This is its protection as it goes through its metamorphosis into a butterfly.

A very fascinating thing occurs in that chrysalis; just as when it molted in the past, the caterpillar is letting go of what no longer will serve it in moving forward. In this case, it will produce an enzyme that will dissolve all its tissues, while at the same time it will save the important things it developed as a caterpillar that will now help it transform into a butterfly. Science refers to these parts as "imaginal discs," and each disc will grow into a specific part it will need as a butterfly. The imaginal discs will then use the protein from the dissolved tissues to start duplicating the cells of the imaginal discs to create the butterfly's eyes, legs, wings, etc.

After the butterfly is formed in its chrysalis, in about ten to fourteen days, it will emerge into the world with a whole new look—it now has wings to fly.

We are much like the caterpillar turning into a butterfly. Every once in a while, we feel discomfort in our old skin because a change is occurring within us. We shed the old skin of what no longer serves us so we can grow into a better version of ourselves. We go through multiple steps of shedding what no longer serves us until, one day, we long for something greater than we have known before. All our "imaginal discs," which we were developing throughout our life, are now ready to transform into what we came here to do. It is a deep longing that is going to cause us to take risks and step into places unknown, all so we can fly.

As Elizabeth Appell once wrote, "The day came when the risk to remain tight in the bud was more painful than the risk it took to blossom."

The caterpillar will never be able to fly if it stays a caterpillar. To embrace what is emerging in you, you must decide to risk being transformed into the life you have imagined. Embrace that part of you that is ready to make that change. Like the caterpillar's metamorphosis, that change is everything you have been preparing yourself for in this lifetime. It is time for you to fly! Your exclamation point life is waiting for you.

EXERCISE

Where in your life have you seen stages like those of the caterpillar?

_____

_____

_____

_____

Are you ready to build your own chrysalis of transformation?

_____

If not, what fears are holding you back?

_____

_____

_____

_____

How can you repattern those fears into beliefs that help you move forward?

_____

_____

_____

_____

SIGN ME UP!

In Chapter 2, I shared a story of my experience in learning about a concert zither, a German folk instrument. Initially, I allowed my inner critic to hold me back from learning how to play the zither. It wasn't until four years after my first introduction to the zither and attending multiple zither concerts, that one conversation shifted my thinking. Like the caterpillar turning into a butterfly, I was ready to leave the ideas that no longer served me behind and grow into my dream of playing the zither.

One day, I was having lunch with my parents. In the midst of the conversation, my father mentioned that the German American Heritage Center (GAHC) had received a donation to support the zither ensemble in buying some used zithers to initiate a zither-to-loan program. My interest was piqued, so I said to my father, "Sign me up!" I never could have guessed what wonderful zither adventures those three words would bring to my life, as I finally decided to say "Yes" to what was emerging within me.

I became the first zither player in the ensemble to benefit from the new zither-to-loan program. I learned to start playing the zither within our ensemble and would travel periodically to Chicago to take lessons from a member of the Chicago Zither Club, who was also a zither advocate for the United States.

After a year-and-a-half of playing the zither, I was encouraged by my teacher to attend a workshop in Chicago being led by a master zitherist from Germany. Participating in this workshop was marvelous and showed me what was possible in learning to play the zither. What an opportunity to learn from a master zitherist and play with other zither players from across the country as well as with one from Japan. Afterwards, the master zitherist spoke with my father and me about his interest in visiting our ensemble to teach a workshop for our zither players. A new seed had just been planted for the National Zither Gathering—what an opportunity. "Sign me up!"

Within three years of me starting to play the zither, our zither ensemble hosted the first National Zither Gathering with the master zitherist from Germany along with twenty-five zither players attending from across the United States. The workshops culminated in a Grand Zither Concert. This was the first time in ninety-five years that Davenport, Iowa, had hosted this type of event, bringing zither players together from across the country. The last time had been in 1913 when the Davenport Zither Club hosted the Second Congress of the American Zither Verband (Association).

While in Davenport, the master zitherist witnessed firsthand the reemergence of the zither in our locale. Additionally inspired by our ensemble's unique partnership with GAHC, and wanting to encourage the continued growth of zither music here, he invited me to Germany to learn how to teach beginning zither and how to repair/restring zithers. This opportunity would provide GAHC and our zither ensembles the support necessary to provide current and future zither players what they needed to succeed—beginning zither instruction, zither repair/restringing, and access to new zithers, music, and zither supplies. When asked to come to Germany to study, I, of course, said, "Sign me up!"

Each time I said, "Sign me up!", I was embracing what was emerging in me. Since that time, my dream has led me to become the editor for the *Zither Newsletter USA* with readers in ten countries, the coordinator for the North American Zither Gatherings, and co-coordinator for an international zither festival, teaching students across the country, supporting zither players in all the English-speaking countries, and playing my zither with musicians from around the world.

When you say "Sign me up!" and embrace what has been emerging within you, the universe will support you in creating your dream with what you ask for or something better. When I first stepped into this dream, I had no idea what adventures would come into my life from me being passionate about a concert zither and simply wanting to encourage and grow new zither players.

Like Cinderella's glass slippers, your dream is a perfect fit for you. By stepping into your dream and embracing the adventure, your dream will expand your current awareness and take you places you have yet to imagine.

EXERCISE

What has shown up in your life where you have wanted to say, "Sign me up!", but part of you has held you back?

_____

_____

_____

What do you want to say, "Sign me up!" to today, and what action step will you take to say "Yes" to your dream?

_____

_____

_____

MOVING INTO MAGIC

As you begin to embrace your dream and wear it as part of your life, your life will begin to unfold in ways you couldn't have previously imagined. At the same time, things from your past may cry out for you to hang onto them. In her book *Magical Journey: An Apprenticeship in Contentment*, Katrina Kenison writes:

> As I loosen my grip on the past, as I keep taking one small step after another in the direction I want to go, I discover I'm being supported and guided after all, and that as soon as I'm willing to embrace change, something or someone comes along and shows me how. Magic wasn't something I had to go in search of; it was here within me, all the time. When hearts are open, when love is flowing, magic happens.

Kenison is providing a wonderful roadmap for embracing what is changing in you. You may have fears that pop up as you make changes, but as she says, "loosen" your grip "on the past." If you choose not to hold on so tightly to the past and instead begin embracing the journey you are creating, magic will happen. You can only take one step at a time as you begin building your vision. Your vision is like a beautiful flower. It starts as a seed, but with sun and the nourishment of water, it grows. Eventually, a bud appears and the flower starts unfolding its petals, only to open them in their full beauty at the climax of their journey. Along the way from seed to flower, a power inside is driven to make that flower give its best and put on its finest show when it blooms. That same driving force is within you, waiting for you to give it nourishment so your vision can grow and blossom into your exclamation point life.

As your vision begins to grow, it is fragile, and it needs you to tend it like a new seedling. It doesn't yet have the root system to support it if a big wind comes. Like a newborn baby, it is dependent on you to protect it, shelter it, feed it, and love it. Your dream needs your loving care.

You may feel you lack the skills to accomplish certain parts of your vision. Just go as far as you can see to go, and then the next step will appear. Go forward scared and unskilled. Uncertainty is a natural part of growth. You will learn and you will grow even deeper roots because of the experiences you will walk through to get there. The more you step into your vision and build it, the stronger it will become within you. This is the magic Kenison talks about. It is where you will discover your innate knowingness that is helping to guide your way in creating the most brilliant version of you. What you long for has never been outside of you. It has always been inside you, waiting for you to discover your dream and bring it forth into the world.

EXERCISE

What steps can you take to feed, protect, and love your dream?

_____
_____
_____

What parts of you feel scared and unskilled as you try to move forward?

_____
_____
_____

What can you do to help yourself take a step forward anyway?

_____
_____
_____

WEARING YOUR DREAM

Part of embracing your dream is to wear your dream. No longer are you just trying it on for size. Everything you do from this point forward is magnetized by your dream if you feed it, nourish it, and continue to notice what you are noticing.

What do I mean by magnetizing your dream? As you wear it and believe it with every fiber of your being, you will start attracting people, things, and situations that will support the next step in your journey. When it happens, there is no need to be afraid. It comes as God's gift to you for stepping into your vision. It is up to you to recognize and respond to the gift as it comes to you, just like I did when I decided to play the zither and said, "Sign me up!" The opportunities will come; it is up to you to say, "Yes" to them when they come.

So what can those opportunities look like when they come? Let me give you a personal example. I had been wearing my dream of being an author, although I had not yet started writing my book. On the last day of a week-long conference I had been attending, a woman I had not spoken with came up to me and said, "I understand you are writing a book." Because I fully embraced my dream, my response was, "Yes, I am." She then shared information with me that opened the door for me to publish my first book.

Had I not been wearing my dream, my answer to her might have been, "Well, I've thought about maybe writing a book, but I'm just not sure if I should really try. That would mean a lot of work, and what if no one wants to read it?" Then her response to me would have been quite different; it would have closed the door on the conversation, and I would not have been given the next step in making the publishing of my first book possible.

Confidence comes with embracing your dream. Your vision is all yours, and no one holds the vision you have for your life better than you. Your life is waiting for you to create magnificent things. Embrace it, love it, nourish it, and when someone or something shows up in your life and hands you the key to the next step in your journey, embrace it and have gratitude for what has just been given to you.

My dream of writing a book to inspire others waited nearly twenty years for me to embrace and wear it. It was not until I fully embraced it, owned it as mine, and wore it, that the dream turned into a reality and I received full support in its creation. I had to follow the steps, one at a time, not always knowing where the next step would lead, but trusting that God was fully leading me in my pursuit.

Now, as you choose what steps to take with your vision, ask yourself, "Is this something that will help move my vision forward," or "Does this activity match my dream?" If your vision is to be healthy and fit, and you have the choice to eat a pint of ice cream or a salad, what would the person of your vision choose?

Because your vision is new, you need to tend to it often and pause to ask important questions; otherwise, the gravitational pull to do what you have done previously will hold you back. The key is to become more aware of the choices you make.

EXERCISE

What does wearing your dream feel like to you?

_____

_____

_____

What types of things do you notice coming into your life when you wear your dream?

_____

_____

_____

What steps have you created to help you keep moving forward with your vision?

_____

_____

_____

TAKING TIME TO CELEBRATE YOUR WIN

In a blog post on lifehack.org, Jenny Marchal states:

> The key to success is realizing that your big goals aren't going to happen overnight, in the next week or maybe even in the next year but this is okay. We tend to focus on the end goals rather than the small and significant steps we take to get us to that goal. Therefore, it's important to acknowledge and celebrate small wins. The problem with not doing this is we end up diminishing our motivation and motivation is what keeps us on the right path and gives us the strength to soldier on to the top of the mountain.

As you go through the rest of this book, take time to pause and celebrate all that you are learning along your path to creating your exclamation point life. Appreciation and acknowledgment are key.

Making the changes necessary to live your life more fully requires bold steps, and you are taking them! Give yourself a pat on the back. Treat yourself with something that empowers the vision you desire for your life.

I empowered myself by creating my first business card with what I envisioned for me in that moment. It made me feel proud of the choices I was making for myself, even if I had not yet accomplished everything on that business card. Every time I needed a reminder of what I was building, I would pull out that card and acknowledge all I had done to build that vision. It gave me the motivation to keep moving forward as I repatterned my life.

I am celebrating this win with you. You are the one making the choice to change how you view circumstances and then turn them into opportunities. You are the one setting yourself free from what has held you back in the past. You are the one discovering what is emerging within you. Congratulations on coming this far!

EXERCISE

How are you looking at your life differently up to this point?

_____

_____

_____

_____

_____

_____

What can you do to acknowledge the small wins toward your vision?

_____

_____

_____

SUMMARY

In this chapter, we learned about metamorphosis and how to embrace what is emerging within you—the part ready to make a change. Like the caterpillar that turns into a butterfly, each step in your journey is necessary so you can evolve into the life you have dreamed of and soar to new heights. This step is about being willing to take the risk to be transformed into the life you have envisioned.

As you let go of what you have outgrown, be willing to say, "Sign me up!" to your dream. The more you say "yes" to the opportunities that match your dream with this or something better, the more your dream will unfold in ways you have yet to imagine.

You may have fears that pop up as you make changes, so you want to begin loosening the grip on your past. Doing so allows you to begin embracing the journey you are creating, and once you do that, magic begins to happen. Your vision starts as a seed, and with sun and the nourishment of water, it grows. Eventually, like a flower, your dream will unfold to open into its full beauty.

Remember, your dream is still in its infancy. Nurture your dream frequently, tend to its needs, and most importantly, celebrate the small wins. Each time you celebrate a small win, enthusiasm builds in taking the next step. So be grateful for all the little things that come. Your dream is just taking root and needs all the nurturing and encouragement you can give it so your vision can grow into full fruition. This will help you keep the momentum going as you build the vision of the life you love living.

CHAPTER 8

TAKING A LEADERSHIP ROLE IN SYSTEMATICALLY ADVANCING YOUR DREAM

"Knowing is not enough; we must apply.
Willing is not enough; we must do."

— Johann Wolfgang von Goethe

In the last chapter, you learned to embrace what's emerging in you as you live into your vision. In this chapter, you will learn to step into a leadership role as you systematically advance your dream.

SQUEEZING THE MOST OUT OF LIFE

Before my mother passed away, she gave me a gift—a toothpaste key. What she actually gave me was the key for how to live my best life.

For those unfamiliar with a toothpaste key, it's a gizmo you put on the end of the toothpaste tube; you then turn it, rolling up the tube as you use the toothpaste. This allows you to squeeze all the toothpaste out of the tube as you go along in a very simple way.

We could view the toothpaste tube as a metaphor for our lives. How can we squeeze the most out of our lives?

So often, we just grab on to something without any direction behind it. A shiny new thing sparkles in front of us so we grab it in hopes it will fulfill something that feels missing within us. This is just like the toothpaste tube; we grab it anywhere and squeeze it, expecting it to give us what we want.

If we keep grabbing the toothpaste tube like that, we may get a result at first, but as time goes on, it is harder to get the result we have grown to expect. We end up throwing out the tube with much of its potential still inside. So it is with us. We all have potential in us just waiting to ooze out into the world. But if we haphazardly go after life by squeezing it wherever we want, we will never live into our full potential.

If, however, you recognize that life has given you a key to develop a system through which you can create consistent, repetitive results, you will be able to use the full potential within you to create your exclamation point life. This *is* the key. In following the system, you will be able to generate more energy, be more productive, and have greater ease and joy, with less effort.

Without a system, we are inefficient, but with a system, we harness the power of our potential—leading our lives with vision, passion, and purpose.

EXERCISE

What are some areas of your life where you feel you are randomly squeezing anything that comes your way?

_____

_____

_____

What have been your results from doing this?

_____

_____

_____

What step can you take today to change this pattern so you can harness your potential in moving forward?

_____

_____

_____

CHOOSING HIGHER LEVEL THINKING AND MOTION

In his book *Leadership Is an Art*, Max DePree writes: "In the end, it is important to remember that we cannot become what we want to be by remaining what we are." In other words, it is going to take action on our part to choose higher level thinking and motion, to choose a way of thinking and doing beyond our previous ways; otherwise, we will remain what we already are. Paying attention to your thinking and habits will be important during this time so you can calibrate your thinking to be more supportive in helping you move forward.

For example, I used to play on a volleyball team. My initial goal was just to have some fun playing on this co-rec team to get some exercise in the winter. I had no super-ambition to improve my playing abilities. That was merely the level my brain was calibrated to. Sometimes when I served, I would get the ball over the net; other times, I would not.

Then one day, I chose to make a change and recalibrate my vision—I now wanted to get all my serves over the net into fair territory to help my team win more games. To do this, I created a system of thinking that would help me create consistent and repeatable results. I started by visualizing the ball going over the net before each of my serves. I was choosing to use a higher level of thinking and created an action step so I was in motion with my vision.

By keeping my focus on what I wanted and creating consistent practice, I developed a much higher percentage of serves going over the net. My team started to love when it was my turn to serve. By recalibrating, having a higher vision of what I wanted, and putting it into motion, I created a much better outcome than I would have with my initial vision. My initial vision would have never allowed me to grow into a better volleyball player. The vision did not have the qualities needed to create better results, which was higher level thinking put into motion.

We can read, study, and go to all the seminars in the world to learn what it takes to develop higher level thinking to create what we want in life, but if we do not have the commitment to take repetitive action on what we have learned, all our thoughts will just be amusement for our minds, and we will still be where we were.

Be bold and take the steps needed to recalibrate your thoughts to higher levels that support your dream. Create a system in which you harness your thinking power and move it into action. By doing so, you are guaranteed to have a higher level of success more consistently and you will be able to produce better results with greater ease.

EXERCISE

What is one thought you could recalibrate to a higher level to get better results than what you currently have?

_____

_____

_____

What action can you take to put that thought into motion?

_____

_____

_____

LEARNING TO ADVANCE CONFIDENTLY

I have a quote on the wall by the entrance into my house so I will I see it every time I go outside. The quote is attributed to Henry David Thoreau. "Step confidently into the direction of your dreams and live the life you have imagined." I use it to remind myself of who I want to be as I step out into the world.

When I met Mary Morrissey, she opened my view to the actual and expanded version of this quote and how to use it as a code for leading your dream forward.

Henry David Thoreau chose to do an experiment with his life in July 1845. He wanted to find out what life was and what it was not. During the two years, two months, and two days of his experiment, he let go of all his habits and studied the essence of life. He then wrote about the experience in his book *Walden; or, Life in the Woods*. In the conclusion, he wrote:

> I learned this, at least, by my experiment: that if one advances confidently in the direction of his dreams, and endeavors to live the life which he has imagined, he will meet with a success unexpected in common hours. He will put some things behind, will pass an invisible boundary; new, universal, and more liberal laws will begin to establish themselves around and within him; or the old laws be expanded, and interpreted in his favor in a more liberal sense, and he will live with the license of a higher order of beings.

Here Thoreau is giving us step-by-step instructions on how to be the leader of our own lives as we move forward. Let's look at each step by examining closely the words above.

1) "if one" means you have a choice whether you will fulfill your dream. To be the leader in creating your own vision, you start by choosing to initiate action.

2) "advances confidently" means leading with your best foot forward with inner strength even when you don't know how it is all going to come together.

3) "in the direction of his dreams" means that in order for us to be successful, we will need to be moving forward, following the clear image of our dream. That direction gives us focus. Without a clear vision of where you are headed, you will not be able to lead your life by systematically advancing it.

4) "endeavors to live the life he has imagined" is Thoreau offering a little breathing room. He is letting you know that your efforts do not have to be perfect, but you do need to give your best effort as you put on and wear your dream.

5) "pass an invisible boundary" refers to all the self-imposed limiting thoughts that have held you back previously. When you take the leadership role in advancing your dream, what held you back previously will not have the strength it once had. You will be able to move above and beyond the shackles of those thoughts because of the confidence and strength you now hold by living a vision-driven life. Once you have fully embraced the pursuit of your dream and are unencumbered by previous beliefs, new doorways begin to open. You will become more aware of people and events in your life that are becoming more supportive of you and your vision. This will happen because the clarity you have with your vision will attract those people and events that match what you are creating. Remember Genevieve Behrend's quote in Chapter 4, "for everything you want, wants you."

6) "he will meet with a success unexpected in common hours." Thoreau is saying that by following the steps he learned in his experiment, you will meet with a level of success not typical for the average person, who is living from circumstance thinking. The difference for you is that you will be leading with confidence and pursuing your vision with focus and intent. You will have risen above self-limiting thoughts and have drawn to you people and things that help you propel your vision forward. The average person could never expect the kind of success you are drawing to you by advancing in the direction of your dreams.

7) "new, universal, and more liberal laws will begin to establish themselves around and within him; or the old laws be expanded, and interpreted in his favor in a more liberal sense, and he will live with the license of a higher order of beings." This is Thoreau's way of saying that by holding to the highest ideal in creating your vision as he has shown, you will be operating your life in a whole new way. As a result, things will happen to help propel your dream forward at a faster rate than it was moving based in your previous lifestyle. What might have taken you ten years to accomplish with sweat and tears in the past, may, through systematic advancement, come together with effortless ease in a shorter period of time. Because you are more open to receiving what is in alignment with your vision, you now have greater ownership or "license" of the understandings in creating your dream. You have come from a place of leading yourself by systematically advancing your dream to becoming a person who can now provide leadership to others in advancing their dreams.

EXERCISE

List any experiences you have had where you stepped confidently in the direction of your dream:

_____

_____

_____

What was the result of those experiences?

_____

_____

_____

How can you take what you have learned from those experiences and apply it to your life now?

_____

_____

_____

TAKING YOUR DREAM TO A NEW LEVEL

To assist you in seeing this in action, I want to share a story with you about what can happen if you follow the steps Thoreau showed us in his experiment.

As a college intern, I went to New York City to practice architecture. I was going to be there for eight months, and I wanted to take advantage of my time in the Big Apple.

Having been a musician all my life, when I saw an advertisement in the *Village Voice* looking for singers for a choir to sing Verdi's *Requiem*, I thought it would be a great experience to sing such a grand operatic piece of music. I had a vision.

I called the phone number in the advertisement and scheduled a time for an audition. I advanced confidently in the direction of my dream. I had no idea what I was getting into; I just knew I wanted to sing. The choir was the Collegiate Choral, which I thought meant it was a college choir. It turned out to be Robert Shaw's Chorale, originally from the Collegiate Marble Church, where he used to direct.

Up to that point in my life, every choir I had ever tried out for had asked me to sing, "America the Beautiful," which is a great piece of music to test vocal range and breath. Usually, an audition has some sight reading as well, so I prepared ahead of time for my tryout.

I was prepared, confident, and ready. When I got to the audition, other people were sitting there, all of whom were ten to thirty years older than me. Some had stacks of opera pieces with them and were asking, "Which opera piece do you think Mr. Bass would like to hear?" (Robert Bass was the director of the Collegiate Choral at that time.)

I was definitely in a different league of choir auditions from what I was used to in Kansas, but I did not let it sway me. I had a vision, so I kept walking confidently toward it and endeavoring to live the life I had imagined. I had nothing to lose in giving this my best effort.

When it was my turn to try out, Mr. Bass asked me, "Which opera piece are you going to sing for me?" I told him, "I don't have any music with me, so I would like to sing 'America the Beautiful.'"

He replied, "My pianist can play any opera you would like to sing." Even though I had studied opera in high school, my dream for this audition was to sing "America the Beautiful," so I did. This was a "success unexpected in common hours."

I was no longer limited by self-imposed beliefs or what others were telling me they needed me to be. I had put "some things behind me" and had passed an "invisible boundary." I showed up as me, confident and moving toward my dream. Mr. Bass allowed me to audition without an operatic piece of music and because I remained vision-driven, I continued my audition without being nervous.

The pianist began playing the most beautiful rendition of "America the Beautiful" I had ever heard. As I sang, I was completely in the moment, feeling honored and privileged to have this opportunity to sing my best in the midst of New York grandeur.

The next week, I learned I had made the choir. I went to my first choir rehearsal with excitement. When I got there, I discovered I was the youngest member of the chorus. At the rehearsal, I found out more about the performances we would be doing. We were to have two concerts, one at Saint Bartholomew's Episcopal Church and the other in Carnegie Hall with the guest soloists being from the Metropolitan Opera.

Indeed, "new, universal and more liberal laws" began to establish themselves around me and my dream. The old "Laws," which might have said I was too young and couldn't be in the choir because I didn't try out with the right music, rearranged themselves in my favor, and I began to live with "the license of a higher order of beings."

By taking the leadership role in my own life and choosing to advance my dream confidently, I had the honor of performing to a sold-out crowd in Carnegie Hall at the age of twenty-two, meeting with a "success unexpected in common hours."

EXERCISE

What are some action steps you can take today to help you advance confidently in the direction of your dream?

_____

_____

_____

PERSEVERING IN THE APPEARANCE OF OBSTACLES

In his book *The Light in the Heart*, Roy T. Bennett writes: "When you start living the life of your dreams, there will always be obstacles, doubters, mistakes and setbacks along the way. But with hard work, perseverance and self-belief there is no limit to what you can achieve." Bennett is letting us know that living the life of our dreams is going to be an active pursuit. To get to your dream, you will go through everything that is not your dream, including "obstacles, doubters, mistakes, and setbacks along the way." These are to be looked at as blessings to us on our journey. They first come to test us, and then they strengthen our vision.

TAKING A LEADERSHIP ROLE IN SYSTEMATICALLY ADVANCING YOUR DREAM

What is important is what happens when you run up against these obstacles. Remember, they are there to teach you something. They are a gift, even if they do not look like it when they come. Instead of reacting to them, choose to pause. As the person leading your life, look at the 360-degree view of the obstacles and not your first reaction. Once you have taken the larger view, you will be able to collect the golden nuggets the obstacles have come to teach you. Then you can continue to pursue your dream with new clarity and understanding.

I believe the most important part of his quote is "self-belief." For me, self-belief is our connection with our intuition or our inner knowing. It has less to do with our ego and everything to do with what gives us true confidence. Without self-belief, you will not be willing to do the work or persevere. But in choosing to be the one who leads your life with self-belief and confidence, no obstacle will be big enough to hold you back. "There is no limit to what you can achieve."

Being the leader of your life, however, is not always easy; in fact, at times it may be downright difficult, and at times you may feel quite unsteady in your pursuit. Pursue it anyway. Let your vision lead you through the fire. Remember, your dream is an ever-expanding version of you. Thus, everything that is *not* your dream is going to show up in your pursuit to be repatterned. Either the old things will fall away as you let go of your attachment to them, or they will be transformed into something that supports your vision.

EXERCISE

What experiences have you let stop you in pursuit of your dream?

Looking at the experience from a 360-degree view, what lesson(s) did it come to teach you?

_____

_____

_____

What can you apply from this new perspective to help you move into the direction of your dream?

_____

_____

_____

SURFING WITH YOUR DREAM

When I was in Southern California, I went to Manhattan Beach and created a Facebook Live video for my consulting business. It was about the Ocean of Possibilities. As part of the video, I asked the audience, "When faced with the 'Ocean of Possibilities,' what do you do? Do you stand on the beach far from the water, saying, 'No, I just don't think this is supposed to be mine?' Or are you willing at least to put your toe in the water with curiosity? Or are you all in and ready to take a running jump?"

Later, as I reflected on creating the video, I discovered something fascinating. When I first got to the beach, I was at the farthest point from the water. The sand was very difficult to walk on. If you stand far from the Ocean of Possibilities, life will be challenging to traverse, for the Possibility is not part of the sand you are walking on. If you are resistant to growth, every step you take will be laborious. You may be looking for others to lead the way, not realizing that the true strength of the journey is to create your own path to the Ocean of Possibilities. The path may seem difficult at first, but then an interesting thing happens.

As you initiate creating your dream and get closer to the Ocean of Possibilities, it becomes easier to walk on the sand. The sand on this part of the beach is wet from the waves rolling in on the shore. It is very easy to walk on this part of the beach because the fluid nature of the water and the solid grains of sand create a firmer surface. Once you start embracing the Ocean of Possibilities, life becomes more liberating. You are more confident in your step, and you know you are the one who has chosen to welcome the possibilities. Your core essence is merging with possibilities, and you are beginning to lead the way as life calls you forward.

What if you are the person who is all in? The surfers I saw at the beach that day were fully immersed in the Ocean of Possibilities. They went into the water with confidence, and they knew how to navigate the small waves as they paddled out to deeper water and bigger waves. When a small wave came, they would tip their boards slightly downward to go under the waves. They would hold their breaths and come out the other side as the waves rolled over them. The small waves of life were not going to stop their pursuit of the perfect wave. They didn't want just any possibility in the ocean. They wanted the biggest possibility—the one with their names on it. The wave that would give them the biggest ride and biggest thrill.

Patiently, they would wait until the wave with their names on it came, and when it did, they would move into action, ready and confident. As the wave came, they would quickly get on top of their surfboards as if they were in command of the wave. The wave of possibility came and they surfed on top of it with a delicate balance, riding the wave as far as it would take them. When the ride was complete, each surfer would simply start the process over, paddling out to the next big wave with his name on it. Sometimes, the surfer was not as successful on his attempt; he would lose balance and fall off his board, but that would never stop the pursuit of his dream. He would merely get back on the surfboard and paddle out to the next wave with his name on it.

So it is with those who lead confidently in their lives. If you lead your life with confidence by moving forward in the direction of your dream, you will be able to ride the little waves that come your way. The little waves are like distractions in your path, but the person who is all in will simply let the little waves roll over him and keep moving forward.

Like the surfer, you need to be patient in the process, yet ever prepared for the wave that holds your dream. When your dream arrives, you will know it, you will embrace everything about it, and you will be ready to move into action. If you lose your balance while trying to ride your dream, just paddle back and watch for the next wave of your dream to come. You are the person leading your vision so it will come back for you to complete the ride. When the ride of this dream is complete, you will then have the opportunity to paddle back out into the Ocean of Possibilities and dream the next level greater of your ever-growing dream.

No matter where you are in your relationship to the Ocean of Possibilities, you can make the adjustments necessary to be the person who is all in.

EXERCISE

Where are you with the Ocean of Possibilities? Are you as far away as you can be? Do you have your toes in the water? Or are you all in, willing to surf the waves of possibilities?

_____

_____

_____

What is one step you can take today to embrace the possibilities with your name on them?

_____

_____

_____

How can taking a leadership role in your life increase your potential of success in riding the wave of your dreams?

_____

_____

_____

SUMMARY

As you begin taking a leadership role in systematically advancing your dream, remember the importance of how to squeeze the most out of life. To do this, you will need to create a system through which you can create consistent and repetitive results. In doing so, you will be living into your full potential with greater success and less effort.

You now understand higher level thinking and that you are in control of your thoughts and the outcome you want to achieve. Take steps to recalibrate your thoughts frequently so you can keep them on a higher level. Doing so is the best thing you can do to support your dream.

By following and implementing Thoreau's quote as a guide for action, you *will* "meet with a success unexpected in common hours." These tools become a necessary part in helping you to navigate the appearance of obstacles and pitfalls in the journey as you continue building your dream.

Be patient in the process, yet like the surfer, be prepared for the wave that holds your dream. You will recognize what is yours to take action on when it comes. So, embrace everything about it, and go confidently in creating the momentum to lead your vision forward.

CHAPTER 9

CREATING YOUR DREAM TEAM

"Keep away from people who try to belittle your ambitions. Small people always do that, but the really great make you feel that you too, can become great. When you are seeking to bring big plans to fruition, it is important with whom you regularly associate. Hang out with friends who are like-minded and who are also designing purpose-filled lives. Similarly, be that kind of a friend for your friends."

— Mark Twain

In the last chapter, you learned how to take a leadership role in systematically advancing your dream. In this chapter, you will learn the importance of creating a team of support to help you navigate the new territory of your dream.

PARTNERING WITH PEOPLE WHO BELIEVE IN YOU

Dan Buettner, American explorer and National Geographic Fellow, wrote in his book *The Blue Zones: Lessons for Living Longer from the People Who've Lived the Longest,* "Select your friendships carefully. Gather people around you who will reinforce your lifestyle." He also stated, "The people you surround yourself with influence your behaviors, so choose friends who have healthy habits." I agree wholeheartedly with Buettner's advice. You want to choose people who will stand with you in building your dream and reinforce you when you need that extra encouragement. Furthermore, it is important to surround yourself with people who already have the good habits you are trying to create. They will give you further reinforcement as you build your exclamation point life.

Build relationships with people who believe in you. These can be family members, best friends, coworkers, or team leaders. Whoever you choose to have stand in your corner needs to be someone who believes in you and is willing to be your cheerleader when the journey gets rocky.

I have been blessed with great friendships. My friends and I have stood by each other through all our ups and downs, throwing out a life rope when needed; we are each other's sounding board to bounce ideas off of, and we celebrate our wins together.

If you don't currently have relationships that foster that kind of support, that's okay. We all start somewhere. Sometimes we outgrow some of our relationships that up until this point have cultivated unhealthy habits. To create new and more supportive relationships, we need to, as Dan Buettner says, "choose friends with healthy habits."

Earlier, we talked about the importance of wearing your dream. By wearing your dream, you will attract ideas and people who can support you. For example, I knew that besides my family and friends, I wanted to have people who understood the business I was creating, so I opened the door to that possibility and attracted excellent support.

EXERCISE

List the people you know who are part of your support team:

_____

_____

_____

If you were to expand this list, what traits would you like in the people who support your dream?

_____

_____

_____

If you know people you can contact, list them here:

_____

_____

_____

Now create an action step to contact with them by putting a time in your calendar.

LEARNING FROM MAMA BEAR

Many years ago, I was in northern Minnesota on a lake fishing with my family. During that time, we had the pleasure of witnessing a mama bear teach her baby cub how to swim between the islands.

The mama bear led the way into the water and began to swim. The baby cub started to follow and tried to swim behind her. As the cub got farther and farther behind his mama, the cub started to panic and began crying quite loudly. He was no longer swimming forward because he was stuck in his fear.

The mama bear swam back to the baby cub, grabbed it by the skin on its back and, to our surprise, didn't take him to the new island, but instead took him back to the beginning island to start over again.

What a moment! So often as humans, we feel the need to rescue someone and take them to the next place, but that isn't how nature works.

For the mama bear and her cub, it was a matter of life or death that the cub learn how to swim. Mama bear knew it. She wanted her cub to succeed in life, and she knew the only way was for him to learn the skill sets needed to survive. Winter would be coming soon, so survival was at stake.

Your dream is also a matter of life and death. Creating the right dream team will give you the tools necessary to swim to the next destination of your dream, and it will help you stop doubt from killing your dream. You want people who can be honest with you and support you, without taking away your learning. You want people who know your dream is on the line and, like mama bear, will be willing to stand by you till you succeed at building your dream. Nothing is more gratifying than knowing you earned every step of your dream and that your dream team helped you create that for yourself. It becomes a win-win situation for you and your support team.

EXERCISE

What are some experiences you have had or witnessed of supportive relationships?

_____

_____

_____

What can you do to become more supportive in a relationship to another?

_____

_____

_____

BUILDING A SOULFUL COMMUNITY

Cheryl Richardson is a professional coach and bestselling author. I was first introduced to her work when she taught a life makeover series on *The Oprah Winfrey Show*. In her book *Take Time for Your Life*, Cheryl wrote, "Community makes us whole. It heals us, challenges us to be authentic, and…teaches us to love—ourselves and each other…we can turn to those in our community to help us overcome our fear, see the truth about ourselves, and provide the safety and security necessary for us to grow and evolve." Cheryl's use of the word "authentic" is another way of saying we want our relationships to be very honest. We want a relationship to be a place where we can say, "I don't know how to do this," and receive the response of people supporting us in discovering the part of us that does know the next step for creating our vision.

In building my dream, it's been important for me to partner with people who have been successful in the areas I want to create success with my vision. These individuals are part of my dream team. I speak with the core members of my dream team at a regularly scheduled time so we can hold each other accountable for where we are and support each other to take action steps with our vision. We have an agreement to be honest with one another, support each other's visions, and celebrate each other's wins. Others I am in contact with less frequently, but they are very important too. We help each other stretch and grow our dreams by sharing insights and giving each other new perspectives. Like other members of my support team, we also celebrate our wins.

French essayist Anaïs Nin wrote about friendship in this way, "Each friend represents a world in us, a world possibly not born until they arrive, and it is only by this meeting that a new world is born." The supportive relationships we choose for our dream are going to open new doors of possibilities in our life. These gifts would not have come had we not chosen to invite these kinds of relationships into our lives.

It is essential when you begin to partner with others who believe in you that you also become the kind of friend they need to support their dreams. By each person giving of him- or herself in the relationship, all of you will learn much in the journey. These friendships will create the basis of support to help you grow inwardly and learn to express yourself more authentically.

EXERCISE

What personal qualities can you offer to the friends you are recruiting to be part of your dream team?

_____

_____

_____

What qualities are you looking for in your dream team's members to support you?

_____

_____

_____

SUMMARY

As you create your dream team of supporters, look for people who have the qualities you want to instill in yourself. As Dan Buettner explained, you want to choose people who reinforce the lifestyle you want to create and who have healthy habits.

Often, these people are around you, even if they are just casual acquaintances you have met in the past. They can be your friends, family, coworkers, or even people from other areas of your life, such as classes you have taken, people at the gym, religious groups, sporting activities, restaurants you frequent, and so on.

Your dream team members are going to be like mama bear—the defenders of your dream when you don't feel strong enough. They want you to succeed and will help give you the tools you need to see your way through. They will be honest with you and encourage you, all while supporting you to take the next step you can with what you have. They are the biggest cheerleaders in your life, rooting for you all the way to your dreamed destination. Embrace them, love them, and give them the same gift in return.

As you create your dream team, put on and wear your dream. Then decide the attributes you want to attract in those individuals who will believe in you and your dream. Cheryl Richardson says that our support team helps makes us whole. With wholeness comes healing and opportunities to become whom we came here to be—our authentic selves, sharing our gifts with the world. Ultimately, our support team teaches us to overcome our fears and learn how to love ourselves. It also gives us a safety net as we take one step forward at a time in creating our dream. These are the relationships that create growth for each person on the team as we support one another.

CHAPTER 10

EMPOWERING YOURSELF THROUGH MENTORSHIP

"If I have seen further it is by standing on the shoulders of giants."

— Isaac Newton

In the last chapter, you learned about creating your dream team and what qualities you want in those who will support you in building your dream. In this chapter, you will learn the importance of empowering yourself through mentorship and what a mentor means in the success of creating your exclamation point life.

CLIMBING TO NEW HEIGHTS WITH GUIDANCE

One day, when I was going to do my laundry, I opened the lid to the washer and noticed that in the bottom was a little spider who was trying to figure out how to climb the slippery walls. All of its attempts were futile as it kept sliding down to the bottom.

I decided to offer him some help. I had a small piece of paper he could climb on, and then I planned to pull him out of the washer so he could be free. He would have nothing to do with the paper—he would either run in the other direction or curl up into a ball.

In that moment, it struck me: How often are we stuck in a problem of our own creation and we don't know how to get unstuck? How often when someone, who has more experience or a higher vantage point of the situation, offers help do we instead run in the opposite direction or curl up into a ball out of our own fear and then stay stuck where we are? Ultimately, our fear will be what drowns us if we do not open ourselves to possibilities and reach for something higher amidst our fear—not in the absence of fear, but amidst it.

I was once in a situation that was akin to spending years at the bottom of that washer trying and trying to climb up the walls, only to find myself sliding back to the bottom. I did not have the skill set to climb those walls (the barriers I had placed between myself and my dream.) Family and friends would offer suggestions, but I would hide and curl up in my own fear. I was allowing myself to drown. Then one day, when I was almost completely underwater and the discomfort had become so great I could stand it no longer, I reached out for help. I said, "God, I just can't live like this anymore. Show me what I can do to change and create a better life."

In that moment, I knew making changes to create my desired life meant learning new skill sets. I started by doing what I could with what I had, and I reached in a new direction. I started with a couple of online classes on organization. I was learning new skill sets from experienced individuals in order to get different results. I was at the point of recognizing help amidst my fear. Instead of running away from the help, I started embracing the fulfilling things that came to me and letting go of those things that were holding me in a pattern that was depleting me.

By taking these new steps, I felt as if I had been thrown a life preserver; all I needed to do was grab ahold and I would be moved to higher ground through my commitment to learn from those who could teach me the new skills I needed to succeed.

Taking action on my desire for change was significant because once I did, the Universe started supplying me with the level of mentorship I needed to get out of the waters of circumstance. I learned to navigate the old patterns as they arose and repattern them into life-giving results.

This level of mentorship is beyond someone throwing you a life preserver. A mentor of this caliber is invested in you. When you are treading water in circumstances, your mentor will offer you a ladder, then teach you how to climb above the circumstances. She (or he) will never be swayed by the circumstances you are in. Instead, she will be there to help you navigate every slippery rung on that ladder by providing all the support you need. Having a mentor helps you with accountability. It is too easy to fall back into your old way of doing things by yourself because it is a well-worn groove you have been using to navigate your life to this point. Your mentor leaves you all the room you need to create the dream emerging in you; at the same time, she recognizes potential hurtles and provides sure footing for you to take the next step. Through this level of mentorship, you will ascend to living your exclamation point life.

EXERCISE

What areas of your life have you been trying to navigate where you could use a mentor to achieve better results?

_____

_____

Starting from where you are with what you have, what is one step you could take that would begin opening the door for mentorship in the areas you wrote about above?

_____

_____

_____

COACHING IN THE BIG LEAGUES

John Russell, the managing director of Harley-Davidson Europe LTD, once said, "I never cease to be amazed at the power of the coaching process to draw out the skills or talent that was previously hidden within an individual and which invariably finds a way to solve a problem previously thought unsolvable." Russell understands that mentors/coaches see beyond the circumstances their clients are facing, and, therefore, can help them move beyond self-limiting beliefs. This process then allows the creative ideas and solutions that have been hiding beneath those beliefs to come to the surface. Coaching is the key.

In 2016, the Chicago Cubs won the World Series in Major League Baseball after having a 108-year drought. But the Chicago Cubs did not do it alone; it resulted from mentorship and coaching.

In 2011, the new owner of the Chicago Cubs, Tom Ricketts, wanted to see different results for the team. As a very successful investment banker, he knew he needed the mentorship of someone who could help change the team's trajectory. He hired Theo Epstein, who had previously succeeded in getting the Boston Red Sox out of its eighty-six-year drought of getting to the World Series.

Epstein helped Ricketts develop a five-year plan to go from being the worst in the league to being the first. They made choices that most teams would not. They made decisions, not based on circumstance, but on what would make them succeed one step at a time. They didn't just want raw talent. They wanted to be working with baseball players who had character. As a mentor, Epstein knew he needed a team with the right mindset. They were all good players, but by focusing on creating the right mindset in them, Epstein helped them become great team players. He found that players of character would not want to let each other down.

In an interview Epstein did with Bill Whitaker of *60 Minutes*, Whitaker asked Epstein how he determined whether a player had the character he was looking for. Epstein replied, "Find out how he treats people when no one's looking. You go talk to their girlfriend. You go talk to their ex-girlfriends. You go talk to their friends. You talk to their enemies." As a mentor, he knew that for the Chicago Cubs to have different results, they were going to have to do things in a new way. Epstein not only helped Tom Ricketts create a direct path from where the Chicago Cubs were to where they wanted to be, but he was willing to help them make bold choices against the status quo in baseball.

Three years into their plan, the Chicago Cubs brought in a new team manager, Joe Madden. Madden was able to get the team to remain relaxed, have fun, and still be focused on prioritizing their wins. By the fifth year of the plan, the whole organization was so in alignment that it actually achieved new levels in other areas of the game. Its scouts knew the statistics of all the batters the Cubs were going to face down to the finest of details; thus the pitchers, catchers, and the rest of the team were well-rehearsed before the opposing batter even came to bat. Because of this, the Chicago Cubs' pitchers gave away fewer hits than any other team in baseball.

In the last game of the 2016 World Series, the Chicago Cubs rallied after a rain delay to win one of the best games in baseball history. Because they had accepted mentorship and worked consistently and repeatedly to build their long-term vision, they built a winning team one step at a time. Their mentors helped them see what was holding them back and let go of the things not supporting the new vision. Their mentors helped train the Cubs franchise into thinking in a new way. The players started thinking differently and together as a team. They embraced new ideas that were not the norm in baseball. Through practice and repetition of the skills the team's mentors gave them, in that final game, they were able to put their fears and doubts behind them and use the tools they had gained through coaching to catapult them into victory.

Some people may think luck wins the game. That is not true. Author, life coach, and public speaker Tony Robbins says, "People are rewarded in public for what they practice for years in private." The Chicago Cubs, through mentorship and coaching, created their win by making the necessary changes to succeed.

EXERCISE

What did you learn about the Chicago Cubs' mentoring that was important to their success?

_____

_____

_____

How can you apply some of these ideas to your own life?

_____

_____

_____

COACHING THROUGH A LIFETIME

Throughout our lives, we have had people coaching us at different levels, from walking to tying our shoes, and from sports to other activities we do. Once we have learned a skill, if we practice it frequently, the task that was initially a stumbling block becomes a habit—just like tying your shoes: first you couldn't do it on your own; then someone coached you how to tie your shoes; and with repetitive good practice, it became an easy habit.

From a very early age, my motto was, "Me do it." I wanted to figure it all out on my own. I would not ask for help until I had tried everything I could in my own pursuit of my goal. I expended a lot of energy trying to figure things out on my own. If I figured it out on my own, I was very proud—no matter how much time it took. If I didn't figure it out and had to ask for help, I was always sad to have put in so much work, only to succumb to needing to ask for help. I was four years old and learning about my world.

As I grew up, I became more open to coaching in some areas of my life. I had my teachers in school, and I also had coaches in sports. One of my softball coaches helped draw out my potential like no other coach previously had. I was in a new league that was playing fastpitch softball instead of slowpitch like I had been used to. I was striking out at bat frequently and really struggling. The old skills I had developed were not working in this new level of fastpitch softball.

One of the coaches for my team saw my struggle, but more than that, he saw my potential. He would watch me at practice, then help me shift what was needed to make me a better player. With fastpitch, I needed to hold my bat differently to hit the ball that was coming at me faster. My stance was different from that of anyone else on my team, but it was the very tool I needed to succeed. With my new toolset, I would get up to bat and hit the ball. Each time I was successful with batting, I was building more confidence.

From there, I wanted to know other ways I could improve my game, and my coach gladly helped me develop better skills in all areas of playing softball. I next worked on my throwing skills from the outfield, and I continued to learn and grow from there. I'd had coaches before, but not one who was willing and able to draw out my potential and walk me through what I needed to be successful. As I played softball that summer, my goals kept expanding. My coach was there to help me achieve my dream. By the end of the season, after consistent practice in working with my coach, I started hitting home runs and making double plays from the outfield. I had learned the great benefit of having a good coach.

Some years later, I became a softball coach. I knew how to work with the batters who were struggling. From my experience of working with a good coach, I was able to help others repattern their old habits, learn new skills, and develop confidence as they came into their potential as softball players.

So what happens to us when we get older? We had coaches when we were younger who helped us learn how to do everything, and we were so eager to learn. I believe something happens to us after we walk across the stage to receive our diploma. A belief sneaks in that says, "I have learned all I need to know." Then, as time goes on, we tell ourselves, "I should just know this by now." With this thinking pattern, we become less likely to find the support we need. Instead, we stay stuck in a pattern. "After all," we tell ourselves, "I'm an adult, right?" A belief that adults don't need support could not be further from the truth. You need to surround yourself with relationships that provide mentorship to support your vision and guide you through the parts of your life you do not know how to navigate.

Part of my "Me do it" came with me into adulthood. Although I had coaching early on in my life, I did not know the value behind mentorship as an adult. A certain area of my life had been stuck for many years. Bless my friends for standing behind me during that period. Finally, I reached the point of surrendering my situation to God. I knew that my stuckness would eventually kill me if I did not get help. The Bible tells us, "Ask, and it will be given to you; seek, and you will find; knock, and it will be opened to you" (Matthew 7:7).

When I saw the door open, I walked through it. I discovered the mentorship I needed to get me back on track to living the exclamation point life I desired. Author and motivational speaker Jim Rohn spoke of mentorship in a clear manner: "My mentor said, 'Let's go do it.' Not 'You go do it.' How powerful when someone says, 'Let's!'" My mentorship team helped me get over the hurdle of being stuck, gave me the tools to navigate from where I was to new ground, and walked with me through the journey to the other side.

Part of your dream team needs to include mentorship. A mentor is experienced and willing to walk with you through the challenges in your journey. Staying in the "Me do it" will not get you the results you truly are looking for.

Having mentorship is not just an important part of childhood; it is an essential part of your adult life if you want optimum success. Without it, you only attain a certain level of success, and what you really want will always seem out of reach. With someone to coach you, new doorways of possibilities will emerge. You will learn new tools you didn't know about before; you will repattern beliefs that have been holding you back from attaining your dream; and you will develop confidence as you move into creating your dream.

Finding a good coach is important because all coaches are not created equal. When I was growing up, the softball coach who made all the difference was the one who took interest in me, could see my potential, and had the skills and willingness to teach me the tools I needed. He stuck by me until I had success. This is the kind of coach you want supporting you.

As a Life and Business Success Coach, I help my clients through the areas in their lives where they are stuck. You need someone outside of your conditions to help you navigate from where you are to where you want to be—someone who can help you take the steps to reach your exclamation point life. Whenever I speak, I encourage people to find good mentors to help them navigate their personal obstacles. Whether that is with me or someone else, it does not matter. The key is to find someone who has experience and uses a system with a track record of getting results. Make sure you find a coach who is a match for what you want to create—someone who takes an interest in you, sees your potential, is there to teach you, and is willing to stick with you through your success.

EXERCISE

Who are some good coaches/teachers you have known, and why do you consider them to be good?

_____

_____

_____

What are some tools you learned from your experience(s) with this coach that you still use today?

_____

_____

_____

SUMMARY

In this chapter, we learned about the importance of mentorship/coaching. Without mentorship, it is very difficult to navigate the new territory you are dreaming into. If you knew how to get there on your own, you would have already had the results you wanted. Our old beliefs can stand in the way of progressing further. Good mentorship will give you the support you need. Without the support, it will be too easy for you to be pulled back to old habits because they are what is familiar to you.

The 2016 Chicago Cubs baseball team succeeded by operating within a mentorship atmosphere until it achieved its desired outcome. It created a long-term plan to meet its success. Its example provides such an important lesson. Some of the dreams you desire to create are long-term. Staying in a mentorship relationship and working with your coach each step of the way will ensure your success.

Having a coach is knowing you have the backup you need as you progress. Because you develop trust and confidence in the process, new doors begin to open for you that otherwise would not have. You find you want to step up to even greater levels than you first imagined in your initial dream. Now living your exclamation point life is no longer just a dream; it has become your reality.

CHAPTER 11

—ⱳ—

STEPPING FORWARD WITH CONFIDENCE

> "Don't wait until everything is just right. It will never be perfect. There will always be challenges, obstacles, and less than perfect conditions. So what? Get started now. With each step you take, you will grow stronger and stronger, more and more skilled, more and more self-confident, and more and more successful."
>
> — Mark Victor Hansen

In the last chapter, you learned about the importance of empowering yourself through mentorship and the role of a mentor in creating your exclamation point life. In this chapter, you will learn what confidence really is and how to keep stepping forward to create your dream with confidence, even in the midst of circumstances.

KEEPING YOUR EYES ON YOUR DREAM

During the Big 10 Championships 600-meter track race in 2008, college senior Heather Dorniden was favored to win the race in front of her home crowd in Minnesota.

LIVING YOUR EXCLAMATION POINT LIFE!

Dorniden was applying all her years of training as she began the race and set her pace. She was exactly where she wanted to be as she moved into being the lead runner heading into the final lap. Then a potentially defeating circumstance occurred. The person behind her stepped on her heel, causing her to fly forward and land face down. All the other runners ran ahead of her as she pulled herself up from the ground and started running. She was now at least twenty-five meters behind the others with less than one lap left.

Dorniden's dream was to win the race for the team. Circumstances would tell you she was out of the race and there was no way she could catch up. Instead of giving up, however, Dorniden confidently pursued her dream in the midst of circumstances. She rose to the occasion and sprinted the remainder of the race. By the second to last turn, she had passed the last place runner. By the last turn, she was nipping at the heels of the runner in second place. By the finish line, she had won by .04 seconds.

What happens when you trip up on the way to building your vision? How determined are you to succeed in achieving your dream?

Dorniden didn't stop running to think about her options. She knew that moment meant now or never for her dream. She held nothing back to fulfill her vision.

Heather Dorniden's story can be your story as you step confidently into your dream, just like Henry David Thoreau's quote from *Walden* in Chapter 8 described. Heather pursued her dream confidently with focus and intent. She rose above any self-limiting thoughts and applied her will to propel her vision forward. This was not willpower—where she forced herself forward. Instead, this was her will—the ability to come from her connection to her inner knowingness, to give herself a command, and to follow it. It was her connection to the Higher Power within her that made it possible for her will to propel her forward so she could win the race. As Thoreau said, "if one advances confidently in the direction of his dreams, and endeavors to live the life which he has imagined, he will meet with a success unexpected in common hours."

At times, you will fall as you are building your dream. After all, you are learning new skill sets you have never used before. You are like a baby bird testing its wings. At first, you will be unsteady, but as you keep trying, you will become more stable and confident as you build your inner connection and outer momentum with your dream. What determines the outcome of your dream will be the choice you make when you fall. Like a child who falls off a bicycle, will you get back on to take a ride into new destinations, or will you give up and say, "I guess I wasn't meant to have this dream"?

According to the Merriam-Webster Dictionary, the Latin root of the word "confident" is "fidēs," meaning "faith." Stepping forward with confidence means that you are stepping forward with faith—faith that you can live the full expression of your dream; faith that each step in the journey will reveal itself as you go along; and faith that the universe fully supports you in creating the life you would love to live.

EXERCISE

How can Heather's story inspire you to develop more confidence as you move forward with your dream?

_____

_____

_____

What experiences have you had in which you were confident in creating something you wanted?

_____
_____
_____

How can you use those experiences to help you now?

_____
_____
_____

TUNING IN

A friend of mine is a professional jazz pianist. One day, he was going to be performing an afternoon concert at a church. My mom, who was also a pianist, went with me to hear him perform. As he sat down to play his first notes, you could feel the enthusiasm in the audience for the afternoon concert.

Within a few moments of his beginning to play, however, I knew something was incredibly wrong. My mom and I looked at one another in disbelief. My heart just ached for my friend as he continued playing on a piano that was dreadfully out of tune. What started as an afternoon of excitement to listen to great music had just turned into a fingernails-on-a-chalkboard experience for my ears.

But then something happened that quickly shifted my perception. My friend did not flinch as he played the piano. He was playing and singing with all his heart to the audience, as if the piano were in tune. He played confidently and gave his best. In doing so, his music rose above the circumstances until we no longer heard the piano as out of tune.

To this day, I consider that concert to be one of the most profound performances I have seen. By my friend confidently holding a clear intention of what he wanted to create, the universe supported him in the midst of circumstance. We could only hear a tuned piano as he taught us how to tune in to the infinite side of our nature.

EXERCISE

What are you tuning in to when circumstances arise?

_____

_____

_____

_____

What steps can you confidently take to help you transform these circumstances into stepping stones?

_____

_____

_____

_____

ENERGIZING YOUR DREAM THROUGH DECISION

Raymond Charles Barker was a leader and author in the New Thought spiritual movement. In 1968, he published his book *The Power of Decision*, which struck a chord deep within me. Barker states, "Indecision is actually the individual's decision to fail." When I read that, I felt like I had been hit between the eyes. "Ouch!" Prior to reading that, my life had been filled with lots of indecision. I could waffle between ideas for a long time without making a decision. However, I have since learned that you *can* decide to be happy. You *can* decide to have the relationship you have longed for. You *can* decide to have a lucrative and exciting business. You just need to decide.

We make decisions all day long. We decide to get out of bed in the morning (or not); we decide to drive to work (or not); we decide to eat eggs and bacon for breakfast (or not), etc. There is a power in decision that will never come if we remain in indecision.

According to the Collins Dictionary, the word "decision" comes from the Latin word dēcīsiō, meaning "literally: a cutting off." When we make a decision for our dream, we are actually cutting off the choices that do not match our vision. To make a decision for your dream is energizing and will propel your dream forward.

To stay in the state of indecision means staying in the land of fear and doubt. Indecision is your paradigm's playmate, keeping you in the pattern of the well-worn ruts in your life. I wish someone would have said to me years ago, "Get off the fence!" So what if you make a mistake? You will learn to make a better choice the next time. At least you made a decision, took action, and are farther down the road in creating your vision than you would have been staying in indecision.

Theodore Roosevelt, the twenty-sixth President of the United States, once said, "In any moment of decision, the best thing you can do is the right thing, the next best thing is the wrong thing, and the worst thing you can do is nothing."

Raymond Charles Barker went on to explain in his book *The Power of Decision*, "The world of other people's decisions is not your world. No matter how wise and kind these people may be. No matter how much they love you and care for you. They are only maintaining your childhood pattern of indecision, the pattern of leaning on other minds rather than on your own. God made your mind for you to think your thoughts and not someone else's thoughts." Trust in your inner knowingness. It will never lead you astray. You are the highest authority in your life of what is the best decision for you. Allow yourself to be confident in knowing that. The Universe 100 percent has your back in bringing your dream to fruition, with this or something better. After all, the Universe is co-creating the dream with you. You can have no better teammate than that divine spark of infinite intelligence that is already within you helping your dream to unfold. "You are Intelligence, capable of knowing the right idea at the right time to make the right decision."

Successful people not only make decisions quickly; they stick with their decisions as they move forward. They make their decisions in the midst of fear, not in the absence of fear. They know fear doesn't mean they cannot do something; it just means they have not done it yet. They take the steps they can with what they have.

You have the same set of tools successful people do. So today, make a decision on something; then stick with it and see what happens. If you are not used to making decisions, make it something you can do for a day. For example, decide to be happy today and watch what happens. Any time during the day when something comes up that brings up negative feelings, say to those feelings, "Today, I decided to be happy, and I am sticking with that decision." Give yourself the gift of discovering the power of decision to energize your dream.

EXERCISE

What are some decisions you have been holding off making?

_____

_____

_____

What decision can you make today that will help move you in the direction of your dream?

_____

_____

_____

What tools can you use to help you stay with your decision?

_____

_____

_____

PLAYING TO THE BEAT OF YOUR OWN DRUMMER

When I was in high school, I played first cornet in symphonic band. (A cornet is like a trumpet.) I was a good player, but I had my own skill set and my own interest in playing the instrument.

When the time came for district competitions, I decided I wanted to perform a solo. As part of the competition, each of us was given the same piece of music to perform, but we could choose which part of the piece we wanted to play.

My band director gave each of us preparing for competition the opportunity to play in front of the band with what we had prepared. That way we could play in front of an audience before playing in front of the judges. I was the last one in line to play. Every trumpet player prior to me played the same, very fast part of the piece. When it came my turn, I played a beautiful slow part that showcased my ability to have great tone and emotion. You could have heard a pin drop when I finished.

I had dared to be different and play the part of the music I longed to play. Each of us has our own knowingness within us, and when we listen to that part, it will guide us in amazing ways. On that day, I played based on my knowingness, not my desire to fit in. I could also play the fast part of the piece, but that wasn't the point. The point was for me to show up authentically and give it my best. By following my inner knowingness, something shifted dramatically in the room that day. It was as if the music that had just come through me had given all of my classmates permission to be authentic in their own expressions of the music.

Dare to follow the beat of your own drummer, not just to be bold, but to be authentic with the expression that is only yours to give the world. Be confident in knowing you are the only person who can deliver the gifts you came to share with others. There will never be another person on the planet like you. You came with your own unique set of gifts, dreams, and desires. The world is waiting for you to be authentic in your expression, to live the life you have dreamed so the rest of us can receive the gifts you came to give. Step forward confidently, knowing you are more than what your fear may try to tell you. We are all waiting to experience your gifts. Why not have this moment be the moment.

EXERCISE

Take a moment to put your hands over your heart and take in a deep breath of gratitude. As you exhale, let go of anything keeping you from the love in your heart. Continue with the breathing exercise until you feel the love grow in your heart. Then ask your inner knowingness, "How may I express my true self in the world?" Write down the answer you receive.

_____

_____

_____

Do this exercise as often as you desire to help you connect to your inner knowingness on a regular basis.

VISUALIZING YOUR SUCCESS

Maxwell Maltz was an American cosmetic surgeon who wrote about a system of ideas that could help individuals improve their self-images. In his book *The Magic Power of Self-Image Psychology*, Maltz states, "Step out on the stage of life.... Remember that you have a good part, the best you've ever had and you will be a success.... You may be nervous in the spotlight.... You may miss your cues at first.... Don't let it bother you...see yourself as the kind of person you want to be and resolve to make yourself that kind of person." Maltz is advising us not to be afraid of expressing ourselves in the world. Show up—this is the time for your part in the script. Your whole life has been preparing you for it. The Universe has given you a good role to play in the script, and because you show up to do your part, it is guaranteed to be a success.

Yes, there will be times when you might be afraid to give something new a try. You may misstep as you learn the dance of a new skill. Don't let it hold you back. It is just part of the learning curve of gaining the new skills that will propel your dream forward. Just keep showing up to the stage of life and keep honing your skills and craft.

You are guaranteed success by consistently and repeatedly showing up to take each step in the direction of your dream. You will know you are living your exclamation point life as you continue to dream and grow into the next level of your greatness. You are the one leading others by your example. Maltz further says, "You've got the raw material in you.... Dig out your buried treasure and don't be afraid to show it to yourself and the world."

EXERCISE

As you step out onto the stage of your own life, what kind of person do you want to be?

_____

_____

_____

What steps can you take to resolve becoming that person?

_____

_____

_____

SUMMARY

In this chapter, we learned that stepping forward with confidence has less to do with our own personality than it does with connecting to the knowingness within us. Drawing forth that inner strength comes from our will—our laser-focused attention on our dream.

Stepping forward with your dream will require you to make decisions. Trust in your inner knowingness and decide quickly so you can begin taking action. Each step you take where you "decide" to say yes to your dream will build your inner confidence as your dream unfolds before you.

Be authentic in your expression. Listen to the beat of your own drummer and follow where it leads you. Dare to be who you are because the authentic you is who the world has been waiting for.

Lastly, visualize yourself being successful. Know that new skills will need to be learned along the way and you may not always take your steps perfectly. That's okay. Just keep coming back to seeing yourself as the successful person of your dream and keep stepping forward with confidence that the success is already yours because you have taken the steps forward.

CHAPTER 12

—ɯ—

LOOKING TO THE PAST WITH A KIND GLANCE

"Change the way you look at things and
the things you look at change."

— Dr. Wayne Dyer

In the last chapter, you learned about what confidence really is and how to keep stepping forward in creating your dream; plus, you learned how clear decisions help you along the way. In this chapter, you will learn how to look at your past experiences and see them differently, so, in turn, you can learn what true forgiveness is all about.

SEEING YOUR LIFE WITH A NEW SET OF GLASSES

In 2014, when comedian Jim Carrey gave a commencement speech to the Maharishi School of Management, he said, "Our eyes are not viewers, they're also projectors that are running a second story over the picture that we see in front of us all the time. Fear is writing that script and the working title is, 'I'll never be enough.'" Isn't it true that we project out on the world whatever inner dialogue we are having with ourselves. Is that dialogue based on love or fear? Carrey is right—we don't actually see things as they are because we are filtering them through our experiences and our beliefs about ourselves.

Just the statement, "I'll never be enough," can shame us into old patterns. I call those patterns the "coulda, woulda, shoulda" statements. "If only I could have…. If only I would have…. I should have…." The worse part of these patterns is they leave you still holding yourself accountable for everything that happened in the past. These projections on yourself are holding you back from having a perfectly good present and an awesome future. They are fear's way of holding you back. None of us are without our old patterns, but we do have a choice in what we do with them. Redesign your power of perception or your pattern will run your life.

Take one of the patterns that has been running your life. What if you put on some new glasses to view these old stories from a place of compassion for whatever you were going through at the time? Take a moment to pause the picture you have been projecting into the world since that time. Take the highest view you can and look at it from different angles. What does it look like when you view it differently? What can you say about that situation from a place of compassion? Can you see where maybe you were doing the best you could with what you knew in the moment?

I once had a situation where I was keeping someone at a distance because I was projecting the image that I was right and the person was lying to me. Even in my self-righteous moment, deep down, I didn't want to feel that way, but it was a pattern I had allowed myself to play in. Then one day, I stopped the pattern and said, "What if I'm wrong? What if the other person has been completely honest with me?" That was a big shift in perception, and it changed everything about my relationship with the other person. When I took a moment to pause and change my perception, I determined that maybe I was not looking at the situation with a clear set of eyes.

Once I released my need to be "right," I learned that the entire story was my projection and the other person had been honest from the beginning. I then chose to look closely at the tangled web of the pattern I had created and been living in. I asked myself, "What lessons do I need to learn from this experience?" I learned those lessons, forgave myself, and created a new action plan for when the pattern might try to show up again. Compassion for yourself and others is the key. Have compassion, learn the gift of the lesson, and move forward.

EXERCISE

Be willing to take an honest look. What is one thing you know you have been projecting over the images you see in your life?

_____

_____

_____

What is a step you can take today to have compassion for yourself and discover the gift the lesson has for you?

_____

_____

_____

Now, let the pattern go with gratitude because you have learned the lesson from the experience.

DROWNING IN PAST PERCEPTIONS

As you grow in building your dream, your old perceptions of yourself will begin to surface. The good news is you are growing and those old beliefs are merely coming up to be repatterned. So, instead of dreading them as they come up, embrace the opportunity to change them into your allies.

One time, I was at a day-long special training with one of my mentors, Mary Morrissey. As part of the training, Mary asked us to remember something from our childhood that made us proud. The exercise's ultimate goal would be to bring the lesson of our childhood into the present to empower us.

While some people were remembering stories of piano recitals and learning to ride a bicycle, an emotionally charged experience from my childhood came bubbling up to the surface. I hadn't thought about it for years, but now there it was, waiting to be repatterned.

It was the summer before sixth grade, and we were having heavy rains. My best buddy lived across the street, and the two of us decided to slide around the water in my backyard. After a while, we got bored and decided to see what else was happening in the neighborhood. I grew up in an area that had open storm sewers, and at the end of the street, the open sewer would go into a tunnel. Even though I knew I was not supposed to go anywhere near the tunnel in rain, that's where my friend and I ended up.

The street was completely flooded, and the water was up to the top of my boots. Some junior high boys were taunting us to get in the open sewer's water near the tunnel's entrance. They had inner tubes and were having fun with the rushing water. My mom always told us to stay away from the sewer, so I was scared.

All of a sudden, the water that had been up to the top of my boots was gone. With that, I began seeing very large whirlpools forming by the tunnel entrance as the water was being sucked from the street into the tunnel. We tried warning the older boys to stay away from the tunnel entrance, but they would not listen. One boy chose to float on top of his inner tube just above the tunnel opening.

The boy was sucked down in a whirlpool, but he got lucky because his chin caught the top of the tunnel. His arm was flailing in the air for help while his head was underwater. My friend, who was smaller than me, grabbed his arm. But I heard the voice of my mom telling me, "If ever you see someone go down in the tunnel, never grab on to them because they will take you down with them."

Instead, I screamed at the older boys for help because their friend was drowning. At first, they thought I was kidding, but then they realized the situation was urgent. They helped him to get his mouth above water so he could breathe.

I was scared beyond words, but I knew we needed adult help, so I stopped two cars and begged for help. One person was a lifeguard and the other was a nurse—the perfect two people for the situation at hand. They ultimately saved his life.

Much good happened that day. I could see God's hand in everything. The boy who nearly drowned had taken his asthma medication just thirty minutes prior, which saved him from suffocation. My friend grabbed his arm and initially kept him from fully going into the tunnel until his stronger friends could help pull his head above water. I stopped the cars that had the best two people he could have asked for to rescue him. After the boy recovered, he became a changed person with a kinder heart.

With all of that to be grateful for, my mind had been projecting a story over what I had seen. In my mind, I had done the wrong thing. The story I told myself was that I should have grabbed his arm because I was closest.

For over forty years, I had been drowning in the perception that I had done the wrong thing. Now that memory came up in this workshop to be repatterned. This was my opportunity to start looking at the situation with a fresh set of eyes. When I did so, I recognized parts of the story I had never allowed myself to see before. I had been a very courageous eleven-year-old every step of the way. I knew I wasn't to grab his hand and that I could not have served him best by doing so. I got his friends to help; they were stronger and could help him get his head out of the water. I then went and summoned the adult help needed to save his life.

As we worked through the workshop exercise, the question was asked, "What is a lesson you learned from this experience that you can bring forward to help you now?" What came to me in that moment was how powerful I am. When you are building your dream, you create the vision of what you would love to create, and then you take the steps you can with what you have to bring that dream into a reality and let the Universe support you in the process.

My dream that day was to save that boy's life. I took the steps I could with what I had and the Universe supported that dream. First, the teenage boys came to lift their friend's head out of the water. Next, the first adult I stopped was a lifeguard and the second was a nurse.

LOOKING TO THE PAST WITH A KIND GLANCE

This was my first conscious experience of building a dream and watching it come to fruition, even in the midst of circumstances. I did the job the Universe needed of me that day, and now I have had the honor of repatterning that event into a powerful tool of my own transformation. I am so grateful to my eleven-year-old self for being exactly where I was supposed to be to fulfill my role in helping save a young man's life.

EXERCISE

What insights has my story given you regarding some of the projections you have been running over your own story?

_____

_____

_____

How can you update the story you have been telling yourself to empower you now?

_____

_____

_____

DEVELOPING A FORGIVENESS PRACTICE

M. Ted Morter, Jr. was a chiropractor who developed a technique called Bio-Energetic Synchronization Technique (B.E.S.T.) He taught about using your own beliefs, thoughts, and memory to create a healthy body. In his book *Dynamic Health,* he wrote about a three-part practice to forgiveness and would recommend doing this practice before bed as you review your day. Its purpose was to give you the opportunity to resolve any outstanding forgiveness that needed to be done instead of letting it fester in the body and create illness patterns. Morter says the three parts are: "1) Forgive the other person for any harm he or she may have done to you that day. 2) Forgive yourself for any harm you may have done to yourself or to anyone else. 3) Give the other person permission to forgive you for any harm you may have caused him/her."

What I see in Morter's forgiveness practice is again that need to look to the past with a kind eye. When you forgive someone, that does not mean you are approving of the "wrong" that was done to you. It simply means you are releasing it so the situation no longer holds power over you. When you forgive others, look at them with that kind eye. They are also vulnerable people who may be caught up in their own patterns and have simply vented their stuff on you.

Often, if you have not done something to provoke the response in the other person and he (or she) is projecting his angst at you, it has less to do with you and more to do with how he is managing his own life. I have seen this frequently in the coaching I have done with others. Often, the person vents his stuff at you because you may be the only safe place he has.

Forgiving yourself is the second step, because you may have gone into automatic reaction and/or vented your own frustrations over circumstances on to someone else. This can be some of the toughest forgiveness work you will ever do. We often hold ourselves to a standard we do not hold others to. Look at yourself with a kind eye instead of creating more judgment over the situation. What was it in the situation that generated a response in you? Perhaps it was an old pattern coming up for repatterning. Look at what it came to teach you; then forgive yourself for choosing to respond the way you did.

The third step is giving the other person permission to forgive you. It usually takes two to tango in an argument or disagreement; it is rarely one-sided. This forgiveness gives us the opportunity to create a different perception of the situation and to recognize that perhaps we contributed, even unknowingly, to the situation that occurred. The other person probably came from a different vantage point than you, and by giving the other person permission to forgive you, you can help reduce the distress from being larger than life to a very small amount. Quite simply, it completes any loose ends to the situation. This third step is very important; without it, the forgiveness process is not complete. You want to be able to come away from the whole forgiveness process with an inner calm about the situation. If you have a feeling that you want to get even, then you have not completed the process. Be kind to yourself and go through the steps until you feel the charge in your physiology is gone. You will know when it is because you will feel lighter and at peace.

EXERCISE

Who is someone you need to forgive and what do you want to forgive him or her for?

_____

_____

_____

Forgive that person now.

What do you need to forgive yourself for in that situation?

_____

_____

_____

Forgive yourself now.

What are you learning from giving the other person permission to forgive you?

_____

_____

_____

Give that person permission to forgive you.

FORGIVING FROM THE DEPTH OF YOUR BEING

A friend of mine was a minister when I met him. He was just under seven feet and is the biggest teddy bear I have ever met, with a kind heart and a giving soul.

That had not always been the case for him. In his youth, he'd walked a very colored path of drug and alcohol addictions. Sometimes, he would wake up in a gutter and not have any idea how he got there. Other times, he would go in and out of jail. Some would have even called him a hustler. When he hit rock-bottom, he joined Alcoholics Anonymous to help him create a better life through sobriety.

On his first-year anniversary of being sober, my friend was celebrating with his parents. His father told him how proud he was of him. That was the proudest moment of his young life.

An hour later, his dad went out to local bar to pick up a beer for himself and a Coke for his wife. He never returned. Three young men came into the bar to rob it. They killed three people and severely injured three more. My friend's dad was one of those who died that night. All three young men were sent to prison for life. My friend was twenty-one at the time, and his dad's killers were seventeen.

This situation provided such a temptation for my friend to go back to his old ways and seek revenge. He would wake up at night angry because he hadn't evened the score, but then he would hear a still small voice inside say, "You're not this way anymore."

Life went on for my friend and for those who had killed his dad; they were in jail for life. My friend moved away from the area and tried to put the whole thing out of his mind, yet at times something would happen that would stir up old emotions, causing him to weep.

Time marched on for all who were scarred by the event. One of the convicted men had initially been very angry when he went to prison; he got into a lot of fights and spent time in solitary confinement, but eventually, time changed him. He got his GED and started taking college courses. One of his teachers said he was a smart boy who had just gotten caught up in a no-win situation. Being in prison for life, he had reached the point where he didn't care whether he lived or died. He knew he would never get out, so he was just trying not to get consumed by prison life. He felt like he was at the end of his rope.

Meanwhile, nearly three decades later, my friend moved back home and began preaching at a local church. He often preached about forgiveness, but now he knew he needed to practice what he preached. It was time for him to forgive those who had killed his father.

Shortly after he made this decision, something happened. The court reviewed one man's case and discovered that the authorities had withheld information in regards to him. He had always said he was just the lookout and not one of the robbers. The judicial system had a choice; did it want to retry him or set him free?

When the news got out, reporters asked my friend whether the man should be set free. My friend said, "Yes, it is time." Then he told the reporters, "If he needs a place to live, he can come stay with me."

This is when the healing began for the two men. The inmate heard about the offer and wrote my friend a letter, thanking him for his courage.

When the two men met behind bars a few weeks later, all the years melted between them. For my friend, the man who stood before him was no longer this angry punk he remembered. Now he was a forty-five-year-old man who was soft-spoken and wore glasses. They spoke for several hours, and the inmate expressed his regret and apologized to my friend. My friend only had one question that had been nagging him about the fateful night. "As the lookout, why didn't you run and knock on someone's door?" The inmate told him, "I was just trying to save my own butt at the time."

My friend completely understood this response. He had once been an arrogant and angry young man himself. The two men no longer seemed so different from one another. They had an immediate connection because my friend knew he could have easily done the same in his youth.

My friend forgave this man for the part he had played in his father's death. My friend shared with me that this man had made a huge mistake and that it had caused him a great deal of pain. But then he said to me, "But when do we say when? When do we say enough?"

My friend lobbied the county attorney not to retry the case. The decision was made to set a plea bargain for a lesser degree.

Some years later, the inmate was set free with my friend by his side, helping him learn how to acclimate to a society he had never known. He had never driven a car, used an ATM, learned how to swim, or used a computer. He was scared, but he now had a friend who believed in him. He moved in with my friend and learned how to enter life as a free person once again.

Through forgiveness, they both were given a new lease on life. With compassion and the willingness to walk side by side through each other's pain, they discovered peace within themselves to a level neither man had ever known before. Their unlikely friendship transformed them. Forgiveness was the key that set them both free.

EXERCISE

Forgiveness does not mean that you condone the action that hurt you, nor that you need to put yourself in situations of further abuse or danger. It simply means you free yourself from resentment and no longer keep the old perceptions that hold you hostage to the past. Forgiveness is the gift you give yourself.

What can you learn from my friend's story that sheds a light in an area of your life still needing forgiveness?

_____

_____

What action step can you take to start transforming this past hurt, including granting the forgiveness that will set you free?

_____

_____

_____

TRANSFORMING YOUR VIEW OF FORGIVENESS

In 1990, during an episode of *The Oprah Winfrey Show*, Oprah's guest was Dr. Gerald Jampolsky, MD, the author of *Forgiveness: The Greatest Healer of All*. During that episode, Dr. Jampolsky gave a definition of forgiveness that Oprah said transformed her life. When Oprah asked Dr. Jampolsky what he meant by "The secret of true happiness is forgiveness," he replied:

> It really means letting go of the past…of our perception that we need to hold a grievance the rest of our lives…. It really is a willingness to see the person in the light of love rather than in the action that happened…letting go of the past that we thought we wanted. We can't really change that past, so it means really releasing the negative perception of it and coming back to the present.

Oprah has since talked about that transformational moment and what she took away from Dr. Jampolsky's interview. She says, "Forgiveness is giving up the hope that the past could be any different."

Those words came to me at a time I really needed to hear them; they transformed my forgiveness practice.

How often do you hold back forgiveness because you have a belief that forgiving means you condone what happened to you? That is not what forgiveness is. It is not about condoning a hurtful event in our past.

What I believe Dr. Jampolsky and Oprah are saying is that when we forgive, we accept that whatever happened *has* happened. What's done is done, and that hurtful event cannot become any different from what it was. When you truly let go of the "hope that the past could be any different," you begin to set yourself free from replaying the scenario over and over in your head, trying to make it a different outcome. You instead accept that it happened, and then you can *decide* what you want to do from that point forward. Remember, in Chapter 11 I explained the word "decision" comes from the Latin word dēcīsiō, meaning, "literally: a cutting off."

Forgiveness is the opportunity to let go of the negative perception of the past and, as Dr. Jampolsky says, "a willingness to see the person in the light of love rather than in the action that happened." By forgiving, the past will no longer be holding you hostage to reliving an old hurt.

Once you learn to accept that what has happened has already happened and you cannot change it, you are free to move into the present and let go of your old grievances or grudges. Forgiveness sets *you* free to live your life fully from this moment on.

EXERCISE

Where in your life can you begin to let go of the hope that the past could have been different?

_____

_____

_____

How can changing your perception of the past move you into seeing the other person in the light of love rather than in the action that happened?

_____

_____

_____

What are you deciding you want from this point forward? Remember: Forgiveness will set you free.

_____

_____

_____

SUMMARY

When looking to the past with a kind glance, it is important to remember, as Jim Carrey explained, "Our eyes are not viewers, they're also projectors that are running a second story over the picture that we see in front of us all the time…." We project our beliefs onto an experience. Two people can see the exact same picture, but they come away with two completely different experiences. That is because we each project our perception onto what we have seen. Part of our projection comes from the beliefs we established when we were young. As adults, we can look back at childhood beliefs with a kind glance and update what no longer supports us.

In the story of the boy I knew who nearly drowned, my childhood perception was not an accurate view of the situation. It was a child's view. When it surfaced as an adult, I chose to look at the past with a kind glance and transform that experience as an adult, with a much broader and empowering view of that situation.

Forgiveness has different levels. It is important to forgive the other person, forgive ourselves, and give the other person permission to forgive us. Forgiveness is not condoning a past action, but it allows us to transform our perception of the event that has been holding us hostage by causing us to relive it repeatedly.

As Oprah shared, "Forgiveness is giving up the hope that the past could have been different." By accepting that what happened in the past is done and can't be changed, you can choose how you want to transform your projected feelings and move on with your life. Forgiveness is, ultimately, the gift you give yourself.

CHAPTER 13

LETTING GO OF WHAT NO LONGER SUPPORTS YOU

"You stand at the threshold of a grand adventure. The extent to which you experience the fullness of that journey is determined by the extent to which you let go of the scenarios that no longer serve you."

— Rasha

In the last chapter, you learned how to look to your past experiences with a kind glance by looking at your perceptions and learning what true forgiveness is all about. In this chapter, you will learn how to let go of what you have outgrown and learn how to say yes to what you truly would love in your life.

EATING AT THE CHILDREN'S TABLE

I had the pleasure of growing up with the family of my dad's best friend. Most of my life, we did not grow up in the same state, but our families got along so well that we managed to spend about five weeks together a year. When I think of them, my memories are always about playing and having fun.

Many years later, after we had all grown up, we decided to have a reunion. One evening, we all went out to dinner. I was sitting next to my dad's best friend's daughter. She and I had a sharp realization together: We were no longer at the children's table. That was now reserved for the kids in the room. We were now the adults.

We both looked at each other and said, "How did that happen?" We had both grown up. We no longer needed our parents to be cutting our meat and making sure we behaved in public. We surrendered to the fact that we were no longer little kids, and then we embraced that we got to sit at the big people's table.

So it is with your dreams. As you grow and your dream evolves, you may not have noticed that you have changed significantly. Then something occurs and you get the chance to see where you used to be. At that moment, you get the opportunity to surrender your old self in exchange for whom you have become in the journey.

Some updates aren't as easy as that to assimilate, especially when you have outgrown a relationship or a job, or your home is filled with things that no longer match who you are at this stage in the journey. Whatever, or whoever, you are holding onto that keeps you in your past needs to be transformed and updated if you are to move forward into your exclamation point life. If you choose to hold on to the things that no longer support your vision, you will not be able to go forward very far because the old things will still have a hold on you. Release them and you will set yourself free to move fully into your dream.

EXERCISE

What are you holding onto from your past that no longer supports your dream?

_____

_____

_____

What is an action step you can take to start letting go of what doesn't support you?

_____

_____

_____

CHOOSING YOUR YESES

In his book *Anything You Want*, American entrepreneur Derek Sivers writes, "Use this rule if you're often overcommitted or too scattered. If you're not saying, 'HELL YEAH!' about something, say 'no'.... When you say no to most things, you leave room in your life to really throw yourself completely into that rare thing that makes you say 'HELL YEAH!'"

Derek is fully letting us know the value of our choices. Many people these days find themselves overcommitted, and yet when they are asked to do something more, they routinely or grudgingly say, "Yes" when they truly wish they could just say "No." You can say, "No." So, what if you were to pause and evaluate some of the items you have said yes to recently? Are you excited about the yeses you have made? If not, it is time to hit the pause button and reevaluate.

Like Derek discusses, you want to "leave room in your life to really throw yourself completely into the rare thing that makes you say, 'HELL YEAH!'" Take a moment to let that settle in. What would your life look like if you chose to say "Yes" to the things that build your dream and create joy in your life on a regular basis? You can have that in your life, but you need to say "No" to the things that no longer support you.

Greg McKeown, a leadership and business consultant, wrote about how to say "No" in even greater detail in his book *Essentialism: The Disciplined Pursuit of Less*. To determine whether to say, "No," he uses "The 90 Percent Rule." McKeown writes, "As you evaluate an option, think about the single most important criterion for that decision, and then simply give the option a score between 0 and 100. If you rate it any lower than 90 percent, then automatically change the rating to 0 and simply reject it. This way you avoid getting caught up in indecision...." McKeown's rule requires having a higher standard for the decisions we are making. Ultimately, what are you trading for that decision? Is it worthy of your time? You only get this day once, so you want to have the choices you make be of high value to you. Why settle for good when you can have great?

As you develop having more value for yourself and your time, it will become easier to say, "No." Start seeing the importance of saying "Yes" to your dream. You are worth your dream and protecting it with "90 percent" yes decisions. Those decisions, in turn, will help you let go of the non-essentials as you build your dream.

EXERCISE

Look at a current decision you are making. What is the single most important criterion for that decision?

_____

_____

_____

Now that you have determined the criterion, how can knowing it help you make a 90 percent rule decision?

_____

_____

_____

Given this information, what new choices will you make?

_____

_____

_____

SHOULD IT STAY, OR SHOULD IT GO?

Often when letting go of relationships, jobs, and other stuff we have accumulated, we can get stuck in this Neverland of "What ifs." We say to ourselves, "What if the relationship gets better?" "What if I just work harder?" "What if I need ten bottles of Elmer's Glue to make a project in the future?" The "what ifs" only hold us in a pattern of being stuck. Remember from Chapter 11 how the power of making a decision can help you move forward with your dream? Indecision is your paradigm's playmate, keeping you in the pattern of the well-worn ruts in your life. You cannot make progress moving forward if you keep yourself tied to what no longer supports you.

During one of my moves, I was downsizing, so I tried to go through everything before I moved to donate what I no longer needed. When I got to my bottom desk drawer, I found a whole stack of construction paper. I paused for a moment to wonder, "When was the last time I used construction paper?" It had been at least twenty years, and yet here it was at the bottom of my desk drawer.

In that moment, a realization came over me. Here I had kept something for over twenty years that I had not used and that held no sentimental value to me. What had made me keep it for so long? What I realized was I had a value system I had inherited from my grandparents. I could hear them say, "Well, you will never know when you might need that." This was based on them living through the Great Depression. I knew in that moment that I needed to update my thinking to support me in moving forward. I declared, "I am fully abundant. If I need construction paper at some point in my life, I can afford to go out and purchase construction paper." I then packed up the construction paper in a box to be donated.

As little as a package of construction paper may seem, it was quite an awakening for me. I chose in that moment to let go of limiting beliefs so I could move forward freely. Once you take one step in letting go and transform your thinking around it, the sky becomes the limit for what you can transform to move into your dream.

What about other things you have held on to for different reasons?

Do you still have your first ballet slippers or baseball glove? What about that item you are still so attached to that you keep it? Is it moving your dream forward, or is it holding you in a pattern with your past?

After my parents passed away, I read an article about taking pictures of cherished items of the past so you still have the memory without the burden later of having the thing. Again, what an awakening—it is the memory we associate with the thing, not the actual thing, that we are holding onto. What can you do to transform those thoughts?

Be kind to yourself as you go through the process, and give yourself permission to learn along the way.

EXERCISE

What are some belongings in your house that you no longer use and are ready to let go of?

_____
_____
_____

What are some of the limiting thoughts you have held about those items that have stopped you from letting them go?

_____
_____
_____

How can you transform the old thoughts into something that empowers you as you let go of the items?

_____

_____

_____

SUPPORT YOURSELF BETTER THROUGH ORGANIZATION

In *Organizing from the Inside Out*, Julie Morgenstern, owner of the full-service organizing company Task Masters, proposed a new definition of organization: "Organizing is the process by which we create environments that enable us to live, work, and relax exactly as we want to. When we are organized, our homes, offices, and schedules reflect and encourage who we are, what we want, and where we are going." When I read that statement, I thought, "What a liberating definition of organization." I noticed that as I read the statement, I felt freer. But freer from what?

Organization is less about how something looks than how it functions. If you have any area of your life that is not functioning well, then a shift is wanting to emerge; once you make that shift, you will be propelled forward with your dream.

Sometimes we get hooked on our old patterns and emotions about something; other times, we just have not developed the toolset that can help us. What is important is to get out of staying stuck by taking whatever action step you can. The Internet can be a great resource for all kinds of tools to help you.

In her book, Morgenstern talks about first analyzing the situation, then strategizing a plan of action, and finally attacking the task by getting the job done. This process is the same with every step of building your vision: the discovery phase, creating your action steps by putting them on your calendar, and then taking the action step. If you organize your environment and let go of what is no longer needed, and then you organize the rest in a way that supports the life you are creating, you will have the new definition of "organization" that Morgenstern is talking about. You will be fully living your vision in all areas of your life—from the inside out, free of the things that have been holding you back.

EXERCISE

What feelings are you noticing when you think about organizing and letting go? Are there any feelings that need to be repatterned before you begin?

_____

_____

Take one small area of your life that is currently not functioning well. Analyze what needs to shift. Create a strategy for your plan of action. (Yes, this means putting it on your calendar.) Attack the task and get the job done. Write about what you learned from that experience here:

_____

_____

RECLAIMING YOUR RELATIONSHIPS OR LETTING THEM GO

As alluded to earlier in this chapter, sometimes your current relationship(s) are the most important part of your life to change. You may have lived in a pattern of how you and another individual communicate for days or years. If you want this relationship to evolve, it is important to communicate as soon as you can after an event has happened where you or the other person is left hurt. Harbored resentments only fester the longer they go on, so you want to resolve them as soon as possible.

If you are the one with the hurt feelings, tell the person the facts of the situation, how it made you feel, and what you want in the future; then ask the other person whether that would be okay with him or her? As you express yourself, be mindful to stick with the facts and your own feelings about what occurred. You do not want to add things that will only inflame the situation like name calling, blaming, button pushing, or hitting below the belt. These things will only create a heated argument, when what you really want is to have your feelings heard and for the relationship to work better for you in the future.

Some relationships are outright toxic; for a period, you may have decided you can tolerate it. In such relationships, you have become intoxicated with having toxic people in your life. You have sacrificed who you are to be with the other person. It is important in all relationships to pay attention to how you feel within that relationship and to be honest with yourself. Pay attention to whether you try to side-step and rationalize the other person's behavior. If you do this frequently, pay close attention to what is happening in your relationship.

Toxic relationships can have different levels, whether they are with friends, coworkers, someone you are dating, family members, or spouses. None of those levels are healthy, but some have more severe consequences if you stay in them. No matter the level of the toxicity in the relationship, you deserve to be in a relationship that fully respects who you are, as you are, and you deserve to experience the type of love that comes with a life-giving relationship.

One time, a friend invited me over to her house for the first time. She was so excited to show me her beautiful home. As she showed me around, I had the opportunity to meet her husband, who was lounging on the couch watching TV. When my friend enthusiastically introduced me to him, all he did was grunt at me while not even taking the time to look at me. That was a big red flag that something was going on in my friend's relationship with her husband.

Like many people who find themselves trapped in a toxic relationship, my friend later expressed to me all the things she would tell herself in hopes her husband would love her. She had spent years convincing herself that if she became what he wanted, maybe he would love her. In the meantime, she would wear rose-colored glasses to convince herself she and her children were okay.

Please realize that many toxic people are masters of manipulation; they will violate your boundaries at every opportunity, while promising you that things will get better. Verbal, psychological, and physical abuse are *not* part of any healthy relationship.

Reclaiming your life when you have been in a toxic relationship is one of the most rewarding gifts you will ever give yourself. You are the final authority of what you will allow in your life. You are worth way more than the drama of a toxic relationship.

In my friend's case, she could finally see through the veil of toxicity and deceit that her husband was inflicting on the family. My friend had been afraid of leaving because she did not know how she would support her family. Once the pain of staying became greater than the fear of leaving, she left the marriage with her children.

Eventually, she created the dream relationship she had always wanted—with a man who completely loved, cherished, and adored her and her children. She broke out of the cycle of the toxic relationship to lead a nurturing and fulfilling life.

The transition out of a toxic relationship is not always easy because you may have slowly allowed yourself to be deceived into believing you are less than who you are. Deep down inside, you know that is not the truth. If you are in a severely toxic relationship and you don't know how to get out, seek help.

You can also use the power of your vision to pull you up and out of that toxic relationship. You may feel a bit wobbly coming out of that relationship, but trust that a brighter, richer, and much more fulfilling life is waiting for you.

EXERCISE

Analyze your relationships. Is there any toxicity that needs to change?

_____

_____

_____

Strategize your relationships. What action steps can you take to change any toxicity in your relationships? Do you need help to make this change?

_____

_____

_____

Complete the action step. What gift is waiting for you because of your willingness to let go of the toxicity in your relationships?

_____

_____

_____

SUMMARY

In multiple areas of your life, letting go of what no longer supports you creates a new sense of freedom and momentum forward as you create your dream. Some of those things you have simply grown out of over time.

In other areas of your life, you have learned how to choose your yeses. Instead of trying to do it all, you now have the tools to choose the activities you want to say "HELL YEAH!" to and those to which you'd prefer to say "No."

Coming from a new place in your vision now gives you the opportunity to determine whether people or things should stay or go in your life. Through organizing your surroundings to match the flow of your vision, you empower yourself to live your vision from the inside out.

Take the opportunity to look a little more closely at your relationships to determine how you can support transforming a good relationship into something even better and what you can do if you have a toxic relationship you need to let go.

Anything or any circumstance that is holding you back from living your vision will come up to be repatterned or let go of as you embrace what is emerging in you. By taking the time to analyze, strategize, and follow through with the action, you are creating a healthy habit that will propel you forward in creating your exclamation point life.

CHAPTER 14

TRUSTING YOUR INTUITION AND IMAGINING YOUR WAY TO SUCCESS

"Listen to your inner voice…for it is a deep and powerful source of wisdom, beauty and truth, ever flowing through you…. Learn to trust it, trust your intuition, and in good time, answers to all you seek to know will come, and the path will open before you."

— Caroline Joy Adams

In the last chapter, you learned about letting go of what you have outgrown, how to say yes to what you truly would love in your life, and what is worth transforming or letting go. In this chapter, you will learn about your intuition and to trust where it leads you. Plus, you will learn how to use your imaginative process along with your intuition to help you create your success.

INNER KNOWING

Dan Millman, American author and lecturer on personal development, is widely known for his book *The Way of the Peaceful Warrior*. In another book, *Living on Purpose*, Millman wrote, "To contact your inner knower, be still, look within, ask, listen, and trust. Instinct and intuition lend their guidance long before your head comprehends. To attain knowledge, add to what you know; to access inner wisdom, let go of what you think you know and you will finally understand." Millman knows that the infinite side of our nature knows all things; however, it is hard for our minds to grasp that when we are trying to "figure it out." I have learned that if I am saying, "I just need to figure it out," I am simply working my brain to come up with the answer. Instead, I choose to engage my inner knower—my intuition—which is connected to the infinite and supplies the best answer.

Millman describes how to access your inner wisdom as: "let go of what you think you know and you will finally understand." So often we block what our inner knower wants to share with us. However, no question exists that does not have an answer. If I have not "figured out" the answer yet, it simply means I have not learned how to access the answer from my intuition. This is when it becomes important to pause our thoughts and, as Dan says, "be still, look within, ask, listen, and trust." Your intuition is non-judgmental; it is there to be of service to you; it is loving, and it comes with a sense of peace and assuredness. This is very different from your ego's thoughts, which can be judgmental, controlling, limiting, self-serving, and make you feel less about yourself. With practice, it will become easy for you to know when you are listening to your inner wisdom instead of your brain that is trying to figure it out; the difference is like the difference between answering the phone to hear a telemarketer's voice versus that of a good friend whose voice you recognize before she says her name.

I had a client I was coaching, who was trying to "figure out" the best course of action for rehabilitation after her husband's illness. She said to me, "I just don't know what is the best choice." I reminded her that there may be billions of brains on this planet, but there is just One Mind—the connection we have with Infinite Intelligence. Each of us has access to it. I told her, "Yes, you know what is the best choice. You simply need to move into a state of gratitude to ask your question, and your intuition will lead you to the answer." As she let go of feeling like a victim who did not have an answer, to moving into a more empowered place of gratitude, the answer popped into her mind and filled her heart with love. She knew the best choice had been revealed to her, and she trusted where her intuition had led her.

Your intuition will show up as a nudge, an instant knowingness, a gut instinct. Sometimes it will come as pictures instead of words; it might show up on a billboard, in a book you read, or be heard in a conversation. The possibilities of how your intuition speaks to you are limitless. You simply need to develop the skill of listening, and then follow where it leads you. Like all other skills, it takes practice to get used to listening to your intuition, but once you have developed that connection, it becomes your trusted companion as you create your exclamation point life.

EXERCISE

Have you ever had a hunch, a nudge, or an inspired thought that seemed to come from out of the blue? What did your intuition have to share with you?

_____

_____

_____

If you followed your intuition, where did it lead you and what did you learn from the experience?

_____

_____

_____

How can you begin listening more closely to your intuition?

_____

_____

_____

LISTENING TO YOUR NUDGES

Part of my vision for my exclamation point life is to take the time to connect with people who have been important in my life and to have the freedom to travel to visit them and savor our unique bond.

In 2017, a total eclipse was crossing the United States. I had always wanted to experience a total eclipse so I decided to look at a map of where it would be viewable. As I looked at the map, I had this nudge that said I needed to go see my cousin to share in the experience. I had never been to her home before, so this was going to be a great opportunity. My cousin loved the idea and the plan was set.

A couple of days before going, I started wondering about eclipses and what people think about their meanings. I had an immediate nudge to call an old friend I had not spoken to in many years who lived out west. When I asked for her thoughts on the subject, she said, "Oh, Anne, I haven't thought about this at all. It has been quite a summer." She proceeded to tell me about all the things that had happened and that she had just moved to the town where my cousin lives. I said, "You must be kidding me?" She said, "No, why?" I then told her that was where I was going to be viewing the total eclipse. We were then able to make plans to do lunch while I was in town.

By listening to my intuition several times regarding seeing the eclipse, I had the opportunity to live an important part of my vision with both my cousin and a dear friend. With both, I got to travel to see them and savor our unique bond. My intuition guided me to a better outcome than I could have created on my own. Not only was I in a location to view the total eclipse clearly, but I got to spend time with people who have been very important in my life. I could not have made that happen by trying to "figure it out," but I could make it welcome by listening to and following the nudges along the way.

EXERCISE

Have you had any experiences in which your intuition opened the door to other possibilities?

_____

_____

_____

What were the experiences, and what did you learn from listening to your intuition?

IMAGINING YOUR DREAM

Dr. Wayne Dyer was an internationally renowned author and speaker in the field of self-development. In his book, *Wishes Fulfilled: Mastering the Art of Manifesting*, he wrote "The greatest gift you were ever given was the gift of your imagination.... It is your domain for creating the life that you desire.... Everything that you can experience with your senses was once in someone's imagination.... It is a power that is virtually unlimited, and it has been given to you as your birthright." In other words, our imagination is absolutely the key to creating what we desire. It is up to us to harness the power within our imagination and bring it forth in the world. If you can dream something, then it can be created. All of this begins with imagination. Just ask yourself, "What if I could, and what if it were easy?"

Everything you experience in the material world has been created twice. Once in someone's imagination and then physically. The chair you sit in, the car you drive, the computer you work on—all of it started with someone's imagination. In Chapter 5: Creating With Your Thoughts, I shared a quote from Wallace Wattles' book *The Science of Getting Rich* that ties in with imagination:

> There is a thinking Stuff from which all things are made, and which, in its original state, permeates, penetrates, and fills the interspaces of the universe. A thought, in this Substance, produces the thing that is imaged by the thought. Man can form things in his

thought, and by impressing his thought upon Formless Substance, can cause the thing he thinks about to be created.

As we imagine, so will we create. Thus, you want to use your imagination to enrich and empower your dream. This requires you to focus on imagining what you would love to have in your life and holding state with that image as if it were already in the here and now. When you add your passion to what you are imagining, it will magnify the result.

This positive result is important to understand because too often people use their imaginations in negative ways, and then they get upset when they get negative results. For example: If you focus your energy on not having enough money in your bank account to pay your bills, and you are continually imagining that being a problem for you, and then you fill your imagination with anxiety about the situation, what do you think you will create? Not enough money to pay your bills.

Your imagination is a powerful tool, and when focused on your dream in a life-giving way, it will create for you wonderful results. When you imagine, remember to treat what you are creating with an open hand, asking for "This or something better." By doing so, you will make welcome possibilities that are bigger and better than what you could have imagined.

EXERCISE

What is something you envision for your life that you can fully see in your imagination?

_____

_____

_____

Take time over the next thirty days to nurture this part of your vision. Spend time with that image when you get up in the morning and when you go to bed. Imagine it with all your senses. What does it look, feel, taste, smell, and sound like?

Write down what your experiences were with doing this exercise for thirty days:

_____

_____

_____

WORKING WITH YOUR INTUITION AND IMAGINATION

I am an advocate of chiropractic and have been serving in the field for many years. I concluded that I could be of great service to the larger chiropractic community in developing its vision, so I started creating images of how that would look: "I help chiropractors create their vision, fulfill their purpose, and live their passion so they can achieve optimal results in their practices and live the lives they dream." Every day, I would spend time creating images in my mind of what that would look like for me.

Soon, I had a nudge to call one of the State Chiropractic Associations. At first, I said to myself, "No, I'm not ready yet." By the third time I got that nudge, I stopped and paid attention. Although my ego was telling me I wasn't ready, my intuition was saying, "Now is the time."

Before the call, I fully formed my vision of how I wanted to be of service to the Chiropractic community. I then called a friend on my support team so I could amplify my belief in my vision and rehearse what I wanted to say. After that, I made the call to the State Chiropractic Association, wearing my vision with confidence.

My conversation with the association ended up being the "this or something better" conversation. I could not have made that happen, but I could make it welcome. This dream became not only an opportunity for me to serve chiropractors, but to serve chiropractic assistants as well. The association asked me whether I would be willing to write a column in its monthly newsletter. I said, "Yes!" This was the beginning point of me supporting my greater vision within the chiropractic profession.

This result all began with me creating my vision and spending time in my imagination with what I would love to create. As I developed a daily ritual of creating images of my dream, my intuition would give me a nudge toward the next step. I was a match for what the State Chiropractic Association's need was. Remember what you want, wants you.

Since that time, the doorways for my service have grown and grown because I have used my imagination to create bigger and better dreams of how I can be of service. My intuition keeps letting me know what steps to take. When I do take the action steps, I get to see how I have simply attracted those people who could benefit by what I offer. I have drawn to me the people and experiences that match what I have imagined with the "this or something better" request.

EXERCISE

Is there a time in your life when you imagined something you would love, and then your intuition opened the door for you to experience it? If so, what did you learn from that experience that you can apply now?

_____

_____

_____

What is a step you can take today to imagine further into your dream?

_____

_____

LAND OF MAKE BELIEVE

Chuck Mangione is an American jazz composer and flugelhorn player. When I was in high school, his music became very popular. Those of us in the trumpet section in band loved his music and tried to emulate it. The title song on Mangione's album *Land of Make Believe* was performed live by singer Esther Satterfield. To this day, it remains one of my favorites because I love its message of how imagination is the secret for making you feel better or finding a way out of your troubles. Mangione's music reminds us that that we always have a choice. If we discover that we are "feeling down and out," it is time for us to discover a different way and move into the land of make believe where we can imagine a brighter world.

If you were taught to stop daydreaming, then this strategy may be a whole new way of thinking for you. Just know that dreams and imagination are what bring vitality to life. When you combine imagination with intuition, you will develop a far richer life than what the "real world" could ever give you.

EXERCISE

Allow yourself to dream big. List five things you would love to experience if you could have anything you wanted without anything holding you back. What would you love? (Let yourself fully play in the land of make believe).

1. _____

2. _____

3. _____

4. _____

5. _____

SUMMARY

Learning to trust your intuition and use your imagination to create success work hand-in-hand. Both are skills you can develop.

Pay attention to the many ways your intuition will speak to you. Sometimes it shows up as a nudge, an instant knowingness, or a gut instinct. Other times it may show up in situations in your daily life, such as in the newspaper, a conversation, or a street sign. Remember, your intuition is non-judgmental; it is there to be of service to you, is loving, and comes with a sense of peace and assuredness. As you learn to listen to and follow your intuition, it will become a trusted companion on your journey.

By following your intuition, you open the door to something greater to support you and your dream. For example, when I dreamt of experiencing a total eclipse, my intuition led me to a location where I could fulfill part of my vision of sharing time with two people who are important in my life.

Your imagination is a gift that allows you to connect your dream with your intuition. By imagining your vision with passion, your intuition will show up to help you connect to those circumstances or people who match your vision. When you use your imagination and follow your intuition, you magnetize your dream so it will attract to you what you want. Then you step into living your exclamation point life.

CHAPTER 15

SEIZING YOUR OPPORTUNITIES

"Seize every day as an adventure and your spirit will soar when you discover the wonderful surprises life has to offer."

— Author Unknown

In the last chapter, you learned how to use both your imagination and intuition to help you create your success. In this chapter, you will learn about living purposefully and seizing your opportunities.

LIVING PURPOSEFULLY

Former US First Lady Elcanor Roosevelt was well-known for being a diplomat and activist. She once said, "The purpose of life is to live it, to taste experience to the utmost, to reach out eagerly and without fear for newer and richer experience." Let's take Roosevelt's advice and live life without holding anything back. Allow yourself to experience everything that life offers. To do so, you will need to circulate the gifts you came to give the world and to do so from the depths of your being. For it is in giving of your time and talents that you receive the blessings of those rich experiences.

Take all the steps you can for as far as you can see, and then the Universe will supply the light for the next steps in your journey. Let go of how it is all going to come together, and instead, embrace the steps you know are yours to take. The world is waiting for you to share your gifts. You are the only one who will ever be on the planet who can share the gifts you have in the way you can share them. What you feel passionate about will lead you. So step confidently into your dream and wear your vision with enthusiasm, for you are creating your exclamation point life.

I believe each of us has a part within that wants to know we have lived well and made a difference in the world. It is up to you to choose to live well and make that difference. It is through your action that this will be made possible.

By choosing to live purposefully, your life will be full of adventure. Your purpose is the driving force within you. It will never be found outside of you. The path is an inward journey. I think of it as peeling away the layers of an artichoke. You peel away old beliefs, fears, resentments, forgiveness, and perceptions so you can get to the heart or pulse of your existence and what you came here to do. Your purpose is God's gift to you, so embrace it and live your life to the fullest. We were all meant to do more than survive our life experiences. We are here to live life with an ever-curious nature and thrive in possibility. Living your purpose-filled life will be the most rewarding gift you can ever give yourself.

EXERCISE

What gifts do you have that you would like to share with the world?

What step can you take today to start sharing your gift?

_____

_____

_____

LIVING AN EXCLAMATION POINT LIFE

This book started because of a conversation I had with one of my sisters after my father's death. My mother had passed away six years prior, so I had a sharp realization that only three of us were left in our family line and none of us had children. As we grappled with what this meant in this time of our grief, the following words came out of my mouth, "I don't know about you, but I plan on going out with an exclamation point!" In that moment, I did not know what that meant, but I did know I was not living it.

Over the next few years, those words kept echoing in my head as I began wondering what that would look like. That was when I began putting into action all those things I had been studying for years, but had never applied to my life. It was time to take some bold action steps if I was going to live an exclamation point life. I chose to step outside of my comfort zone and rediscover the dreams I had buried to find out whether they were still valid at that point in my life.

My purpose in this world is to help awaken as many people as possible into realizing that they, too, can live lives they absolutely love! By sharing my stories, experiences, and what I have learned by all the great teachers who have shed light on my path, I have been able to touch many people's lives through my speaking, teaching, coaching, and writing. I am an example that it is possible to live your exclamation point life.

When Mahatma Gandhi was once asked by a reporter in a train station, "Do you have a message I can take back to my people?" he replied with a few words on a scrap of paper, "My life is my message." Let your life be your message to the world. Live your life boldly and embrace the possibilities that life offers you. This is your life. You get the choice of how you want to live it. Living your exclamation point life is really about whom you become in the journey as you transform your beliefs and circumstances to create a life you would love living. I am here cheering you on. I believe in you and the gifts you came to share with the world.

EXERCISE

If anything were possible, what would your exclamation point life look like? Please feel free to use extra paper to write this down. You want to allow yourself unlimited freedom in expressing your dream.

_____

_____

_____

_____

What part of your exclamation point life are you ready to start today?

_____

_____

_____

INVITING YOURSELF TO TAKE THE NEXT STEP

"The Invitation," a poem by spiritual counselor and storyteller Oriah Mountain Dreamer, begins:

> It doesn't interest me what you do for a living. I want to know what you ache for, and if you dare to dream of meeting your heart's longing.
>
> It doesn't interest me how old you are. I want to know if you will risk looking like a fool for love, for your dream, for the adventure of being alive….

What I have always loved about this poem is how Oriah invites the reader to strip away the status quo of our societal beliefs to expose the deepest parts of our humanness. Our life is not about what we do for a living, how old we are, how big our house is, or how much money we make. It is not about where we went to school or whom we know.

To be alive with our purpose means that we need to be willing to let go of qualities we carry that are not our purpose. Purpose is not the same as a vocation, although how we do our vocation can come from our purpose.

I invite you to experience your life deeply. To explore the parts of yourself you have never allowed to come to the surface. Embrace all of it—the good, the bad, and the ugly. It is all part of your story, and all of it deserves to be transformed so you can lead an exceptional life that has depth and meaning for you. I invite you to explore the depths of yourself and use the tools set forth in this book to keep taking steps forward to live your dream and step into your exclamation point life.

In his book *Flecks of Gold on a Path of Stone: Simple Truths for Profound Living*, professional counselor and ordained minister Craig Lounsbrough writes, "It's not about inviting great things into our lives. Rather, it's about accepting the invitation of great things to step out of our lives." We need to accept the invitation that there is more wanting to be expressed in our lives. Success will not be found in inviting more things to come into your already full life. Instead, you have to step beyond the boundaries of the life you have known. The invitation is calling you forth, waiting for you to take the step, and take the chance to accept the beauty the gift is offering you.

You only get this life once. Why not live it from the richness and fullness of every fiber of your being? Embody the bold new you. Step into the legacy you desire to leave this world. The invitation is waiting for you to say, "Yes!"

EXERCISE

What great things are inviting you to step outside of your current life?

_____

_____

_____

What will it take for you to say yes to this invitation?

_____

_____

_____

What step can you take today to step into this invitation?

_____

_____

_____

UPDATING YOUR VISION

When I was a little girl, I wanted to be a ballerina. I loved watching the ballet and going to ballet class. Then I outgrew that desire and wanted to be a hairdresser. Everything when you are a child is in the land of make believe. We try it on for a while, and when we outgrow it, we move on to the next thing and try that on. It is part of what we do to become an adult someday.

As adults, it is important to continue having that childlike wonder and dream about what you would love your life to be. There are no limits.

I have what I call a "travel size" version of my vision. It contains the high points of my total vision and is all on one sheet of paper. I read it out loud every morning when I get up and again when I go to bed. It helps me to "put on" my vision before I enter my day and reminds me at the end of the day of who I am as the person creating my dream life. I have found reading my vision out loud is a very powerful practice.

An interesting thing has occurred as I've developed this practice. At times when I read the dream, I am filled with joy as I recognize I am now living those parts of my dream and loving every minute of it! As I read other parts, I realize they no longer feel right. When this happens to you, recognize it as a great sign. You have just outgrown the best version of your dream up to this point. Something greater is now wanting to express itself through you. This is the new and improved you wanting to come in.

When any area of my dream feels a bit off, I lean into it. Often, I need to update the language I used in the previous version. Sometimes, my dream just needs more clarification, and by doing this, it gives me more connection with my dream. Each time I go into my dream and update it, I feel an expansion occurring within me.

If you ever decide to take something out of your dream, here are some rules of thumb. Never take something out because you feel you can't have it. Instead, you want to work on the belief holding you back from allowing you to step fully into that part of your dream and keep moving forward. The only time you can let go of a part of your dream is to pursue something even better that shows up, or if you have completed that part of your vision. You want to continue raising the bar with your dream; you never want to settle. So keep dreaming big, bright, beautiful dreams, and live the life you've imagined.

EXERCISE

As you look at the vision you have created, are there areas that need to be updated?

_____

_____

_____

If you have updates or additions you would like to add to your vision, add them here:

_____

_____

_____

MOVING FORWARD AND SEIZING THE DAY

Although this may look like this book's last chapter, it is really just the beginning—the starting point for you to live your exclamation point life. As you move forward with your dream from this day forward, look at each day in a brand-new way. Each day has the potential to expand beyond the day before. It is up to you to keep taking the steps forward, and by doing so, you will have the momentum to move your dream forward.

Brazilian lyricist and novelist Paulo Coelho is perhaps best-known for his book *The Alchemist*. In a Twitter post, he wrote about the importance of seizing the day. "One day you will wake up and there won't be any more time to do the things you've always wanted to do. Do it now." Our time is our most precious commodity. How will you choose to use your time? You can either live the same circumstances in your life over and over again, or you can choose to step beyond those boundaries and truly harness your full potential.

To keep making progress in realizing your dream, continue using this book's tools. They will transform your life if you work and rework with them until you create the life of your dreams.

American aviation pioneer Amelia Earhart once said, "The most difficult thing is the decision to act. The rest is merely tenacity. The fears are paper tigers. You can do anything you decide to do. You can act to change and control your life; and the procedure, the process is its own reward."

Your next step is waiting for you. It's time to fly into new heights and claim the life you would love living!

EXERCISE

What have you learned about yourself that you did not know before reading this book?

_____

_____

_____

SUMMARY

In living your purpose, you want to live your life without holding anything back. Allow yourself to experience everything that life offers. Sharing your gifts with the world is one of the most rewarding parts of this journey. By giving of your time and talents, you will receive the blessings of those experiences and leave a legacy for those who learned from you.

As a person living your exclamation point life, let your life be your message to the world. Live your life boldly and embrace the possibilities that life offers you. Whom you become in the journey as you transform your circumstances and move into creating a life you would love living is the most rewarding gift you can give to yourself and share with others.

In this chapter, you learned about updating your vision as you go along. As you grow, so will your dream. As you complete parts of your dream, you will want to add and embrace new adventures as part of your vision. Reading your vision statement at least once a day will help you stay on track with your vision and motivate you to move your dream forward.

You also learned that life is inviting you to explore the parts of yourself you have never allowed to come to the surface. Embrace all of it! Your story deserves to be transformed so you can lead an exceptional life that has depth and meaning for you. The tools in this book are here to serve you in continuing to step forward and expand your dream to live life to the fullest.

This chapter also challenges you to keep your momentum going forward by seizing the day. It's up to you to take the action steps forward to harness your potential and live your exclamation point life.

"Decide what you want, and then act as if it is impossible to fail."

— Brian Tracy

A FINAL NOTE

—⌇—

CONTINUING FORWARD MOMENTUM AND SUCCEEDING IN YOUR VISION

"Inspiration must create more than just wonderment. Inspiration must create action…. Genuine inspiration creates transformation. Inspiration without transformation is just *American Idol*…. Inspiration must provide an invitation and a challenge."

— Chris Guillebeau

Now that you have finished reading this book, what are you going to do? What action steps are you going to take? What changes are you going to make in your life? What gifts do you want to share with the world? Are you ready to accept the invitation and challenge to succeed in creating your exclamation point life?

I invite and challenge you to take action in the direction of your dream! Inspiration without gaining the transformation is merely entertainment. You can read all the cookbooks in the world, but if you do not actually make a recipe, you will never know whether you could be a good cook. The same is true in succeeding with your vision. It is through study and applied action that you will receive the results you seek.

In the lines below, list the ten action steps you will commit to taking within the next ninety days as a result of reading this book.

1. _____

2. _____

3. _____

4. _____

5. _____

6. _____

7. _____

8. _____

9. _____

10. _____

Perhaps one of these ten action steps is to go back through this book a second time. If you have written in all the exercises in this book, it is time to buy a new journal and start reading this book again. Starting from the beginning will give you the opportunity to read this book with a fresh set of eyes. It is through active practice of the tools presented in this book that you will create your exclamation point life. As you move forward, each of these steps will help you create the next expanded version of you.

In this book, you learned how shifting your perspective opens the door to changing the outcome of circumstances and transforms them into opportunities. You began to recognize what was holding you back, what you could do to repattern your old beliefs, and you set yourself free from the hold they have had on you. You learned how to look to your past experiences with a kind glance, and you learned what true forgiveness is all about. By letting go of what you have outgrown, you learned how to say yes to what you truly would love in your life, you discovered what is worth transforming, and you determined what is worth letting go.

You read this book because something greater within you was calling you forth to live your greater potential and purpose. Now, you have learned how to take a deep dive and dare to dream the life you would passionately love to live. You have learned the steps to advance your vision systematically with confidence, even in the midst of circumstances, and you have learned how to use your imaginative process along with your intuition to help you create your success. You also have learned the importance of empowering yourself through mentorship and what a mentor means in the success of creating your dream.

If you apply the wisdom, experience, skills, and tools offered in this book to your life, then you will be living your exclamation point life and you will transform your circumstances to lead a life filled with vision, purpose, and passion.

LIVING YOUR EXCLAMATION POINT LIFE!

Thank you for letting me be a part of your journey! I wish you all the best and much success along your path to creating your exclamation point life!

Your friend,

Anne A. Pring

ABOUT THE AUTHOR

Anne L. Prinz is an author, professional keynote speaker, trainer, certified life and business success coach, and the owner of Exclamation Point Living, LLC. She specializes in helping her clients create their exclamation point lives by harnessing their full potential and transforming their circumstances to lead lives with vision, purpose, and passion.

Anne started her career as an architect. Her buildings were receiving awards and her work was being published in magazines and books when her life took a drastic turn; her health gave out on her and she was no longer able to work. Although the best medical doctors told her she would never recover, Anne chose to transform her own circumstances and recovered from her illness through the aid of chiropractic.

Due to her own success in creating a life of wellness, Anne has spent the last twenty years working in the field of chiropractic by coaching individuals to achieve optimal health. As a certified life and business success coach, Anne now works with organizations and individuals, helping them build their dreams, accelerate their results, and create richer, more fulfilling lives.

Anne is an international speaker and has been on stage with world-renowned speaker and teacher Mary Morrissey, and she has been a keynote speaker for such events as the Women's Holistic Health Fair. She has been featured on television programs, including *Life and Times in the Quad Cities* and *Paula Sunds Live*, as well as in other media. Anne is also a featured contributor in publications within the chiropractic community.

She is passionate about helping individuals, businesses, and groups rise above the constrictions of their current circumstances by using a reliable, repeatable, system of transformation.

Anne's other passion is music. She grew up in a family with a great love for music, and she started performing in front of an audience when she was four years old. Her family was honored to be the Kansas Musical Family of the Year in 1980, and Anne was also honored to sing in the Kansas All-State Choir in 1981. She has had the privilege to perform under the direction of Aaron Copland, has performed in Carnegie Hall, and has studied and performed music internationally. In more recent years, she has been recognized around the world for her contributions in supporting the zither (a German folk instrument) community.

Anne was born in Iowa, but grew up in Kansas, and graduated from Kansas State University in 1987. She has lived in New York and Maryland, before moving to the Quad Cities area (Iowa/Illinois border) where she has lived since 1993.

ABOUT COACHING WITH ANNE L. PRINZ

Anne L. Prinz helps individuals and organizations create their visions, fulfill their purposes, and live lives they are passionate about living. Although each person or business has different goals and objectives, Anne's programs will help them achieve optimal results so they can live the lives they have dreamed by becoming the creators of their own destinies.

Let Anne help you move beyond living a circumstance-based life into creating a life by design. To do this, she will teach you to use a proven, repeatable, and reliable system of transformation. An important part of her coaching is helping you create your vision, and teaching you how to navigate the gap from where you are to where you want to be. By working with Anne, you will learn the tools necessary to catapult your results in the four domains of life: Health and Well-Being, Vocation, Relationships, and Time and Money Freedom.

Anne recognizes that each client has unique needs, regardless of whether an individual or an organization. She tailors her programs to meet the needs of each client.

Contact Anne and she will help you discover what is waiting to emerge in you.

To set up a complimentary, no obligation 30-60-minute consultation by phone, email Anne at Anne@AnneLPrinz.com or text her with your name and time zone at 309-797-4779.

BOOK ANNE L. PRINZ TO SPEAK AT YOUR NEXT EVENT

Anne L. Prinz offers content-rich interactive events and workshops that take participants on a journey in which they design, define, test, and experience a crystal-clear vision of the lives they would love—lives in alignment with their highest purposes. Each participant will have a unique opportunity to "step into" the life he or she is imagining and feel a resounding "yes."

As a sought-after speaker and trainer, Anne has offered transformational workshops to organizations nationwide and internationally.

Whether it's a short ten-minute talk, a "Lunch and Learn" training, a motivating keynote speech, or an afternoon workshop, your group, organization, or company will be ignited by this training and will say "Thank you" for bringing Anne Prinz to them.

To schedule a complimentary pre-speech phone interview or receive a speaker one-sheet, contact Anne at:

www.AnneLPrinz.com
Anne@AnneLPrinz.com
Mobile: (309)797-4779